Firm, Fair and Fast.

By

Robin Dickson.

Prelog

Who's the Boss?

In every person entrusted to any responsibility there is a great manager fighting to get out. Your natural ability to manage any team, any project, any change, and any product is there for all to see. Your subordinates, your superiors and your equals all bask in the sunshine of your glory.

You are magnificent in all your endeavours.
Your light shines on every corner of your domain.
You are the master of all your faculties.
Your employees know their jobs.
They bring you their ideas.
Your superiors count on you.
You have the work done.
The job is done on time.

How do you do it?
You have the Midas touch.
You attract people.
They like you.

Yet, you can dress them down when needed.

How do you do it?
Are you a fraud?

No.
The intention of this book is to show you, how you can be like the person described above. After many years of grafting in Private Companies, Government Crown Corporations and Sports Organisations from being President of Companies to stacking shelves, here is what works.

Chapter 1

Be careful if you want to be the Boss

The Chinese Emperor.

This story is a short anecdote, which I have used with young managers to show them how to behave in business. Know how to speak to people. Know how to treat people. Be to the point and easily understood. This short exercise stays with the listener. I have passed it on to hundreds of managers, whether in non-profits or Fortune 500 companies or small or even large start-ups.

Try and apply it to yourself. It may surprise you.

Imagine this. While we were fighting the Vikings, or the Romans, or the English, or each other, there was something going on in a country a long way away. So far away that our ancestors had no inkling of its' existence. It was unknown. The country was far, but advanced. So advanced it had already invented fireworks, paper, the art of war and created philosophy. Literature was abundant and the arts flourished.

The Han tribe had taken over the territories and was assimilating neighbouring lands making the worlds largest homogenous area from the East China Sea to the Himalaya Mountains; the Great Wall to the Mekong River.

Sometime fast and sometime slow rivers cut their way East to West. From the mountains to the seas. Carving the land and furnishing water to the Han. Giving life to the surrounding fields, villages and towns. Of these towns Beijing was the home of the rulers. Known as The Forbidden City it was the Heart of the Empire. Home to the rulers of this huge land of Han.

There were many levels of Chivalry in China from Emperors to War Lords to Generals to Knights. Every Dynasty brought advances to its wealth of science. Medicine, War Machines, Astronomy, Agriculture, Hydro, Building Science, Mining. The list of their achievements gives them the prize of being the most advanced civilization on Earth.

The political and economic structure of China was sophisticated. Emperors and War Lords were at the pinnacle of society. The Emperor was the de facto King. It was he who ruled the land. He gave the orders, proclamations, edicts, and the laws of the land. Taxes were levied of course. The Governors of Districts were to collect the taxes and remit then to the Emperors treasure chest. If the taxes were not paid then the troops under the rule of the Generals and War Lords would be directed to collect the non-paid revenues. If the Governor needed help to collect taxes then the Generals would start intimidation techniques to have the excise revenues up to date. The troops would move in and confiscate the goods and chattels of the populace to meet their duty to the Emperor.

The War Lords were the protectors of the Emperor. Some of their many duties were being the police, the judges, the jury's, and jailers. They render the justice to the population. Even if the justice was barbaric, unfair and exaggerated, this was the way it was. Non-payment of taxes was one of the worst crimes. Depending on the amount owed death could be anticipated as a punishment. Torture, stealing of children, burning of homes, villages or towns for non-payment could be the fate of any short-changing. The War Lord was despised on one side, yet another of his duties was to protect the people from invasion under the supervision of the Emperor. The Emperor kept a space between the War Lord and himself for the purposes of tax collection. He did re-join with the War Lord in invasion management.

The Emperor was walking the line between good and bad. He was bad and good. The War Lord was just bad. He had to be to do his job. He just had 100% bad PR.
The Emperor kept all the kudos for invasions, and allowed the War Lord short thrift.

One Day the Emperor was talking to one of his advisors. He explained the fact that he was unhappy with his role in the Forbidden City. He complained that the War Lord was out in the country with the people. Yes, he has a tough mandate. He has to protect the people from the marauders breaking through the North and West frontiers. Saving the population from the theft of their goods by invaders is a primary job. I want to be like that. I want them to see that I can achieve all this as well as the War Lord. I want to go around the country and see my people. The advisor, afraid to disappoint the Emperor, agreed to his way of thinking, but added a reality to the change.
The advisor reminded the Emperor that one of the duties of the War Lord was to be the head of tax collection and meet out punishments. The Emperor thought this over. His opinion was that he would be fine. The Emperor is untouchable and his popularity would protect him. He would delegate the punishments to be inflicted by one of the Generals with me.

The Emperor called the War Lord to the Forbidden City and told him his plan. He would take over the duties of the War Lord so he may save his people in the face of invasion. The Emperor will be in charge except when taxes need collected, where a General under his command will take care of these matters. The War Lord agreed of course. He had no choice. The War Lord asked the Emperor what his duties would be once the Emperor had taken over, The Emperor decided that the War Lord could stay at the Forbidden City and take care of the welfare of the people while he was among the people.

Soon after, the Emperor went out in the country. He fought invaders, and won battles. He gained territory for the dynasty. Enjoyed the love from the people. The Emperor loved his crusades to the edges of the Empire.
Then the time came when tax collections were due. The Emperor chose a General who was very good in battle because of his viciousness and violent manner. He was a kill first ask questions later, combatant. If the taxes were not paid in a timely manner then blood would be spilled. Many nasty incidents, some uncalled for, were committed.

The people despised the General, but they realised that the Emperor, who before, was at the Forbidden City, was now actually the man on the field in charge of the tax-collecting General. The Emperor started to lose points among the people. Questions were asked between the intelligencia as to the future of China.
The behaviour of the Emperor was seen as a disaster. His actions in allowing directly the duress of the populace, even though he stopped invasion forces, were seen as unacceptable. How could this be resolved?

The consensus was easy. We don't want the Emperor any more. He's become a monster.

With whom shall we replace him?

That War Lord seems to be working out well at the Forbidden City. He seems to have mended his ways and be a good guy. He's our man.

Be bad, and then be good.
Don't be good, then bad.
It doesn't work that way.
Short memories affect our decision-making processes.

Our achievements tend to be forgotten with one single faux pas.
If you have to be bad to have results, then make sure that the final objective is way better than the pain of change.
You will never be capable of keeping everyone happy. The reason that you are a manager is that you make the right decision for the goals of your organisation more times than naught. You will make the right call most times.
You can't make the perfect call, as it doesn't exist.
There will always be someone who disagrees.
Make the right decision, using all the inputs necessary and at your disposal.
Fix the problem, and then move on.
Learn from your mistakes.
Accept and retain any faux pas.
Be transparent. Communicate with all shareholders quickly.

Head up, eyes front and resolve the next file.

Chapter 2

How to say YES without causing a disaster within any organisation.

Have you ever been asked by a subordinate for a decision based on;

- Change of procedures?
- Change of work shift?
- Change of Software?
- Change of personnel?
- Change of ANY KIND?

If so, then you are not alone. Everyday, everywhere, managers are asked for some kind of change from their subordinates. Some are sure about their perception of a work blockage, or a procedure, which doesn't make sense to them. Sometimes it is budget concerns where his department has had a budget cut and he feels slighted.
Human resources may have cut salary budgets and number of hires, or even asked for reductions in manpower. You, as the manager and the decision maker, have only one thing to say. The initial answer will always be NO.

Any request received by an employee reporting to you, no matter what level of your management stature will be answered with a firm, fair and fast reply of No. Your answer will be verbal. Your answer will be spoken as the final word on the matter, *at that time.*

Sounds tough, but it is the only reliable, workable response. This is a strategy that works.

The employee's reaction will be one of several possibilities - disappointment, outrage, frustration or even resentment. But you have given the only appropriate response that you can. The reasoning is very simple but the backbone of the reasoning makes good, natural sense.

Once a YES has been given you will never be able to rescind the YES and replace it with a NO without back stepping, losing face, and loss of reputation.

If you give a NO, then follow the NO with a change to a YES, you will be seen as a competent manager who understands the needs and wants of his subordinates.

A NO to YES pronouncement will trump the reversing of the poles of a YES to NO decision. Your worth to the organisation will increase; the boss will hear of it, and a gold star entered onto your employment record.

A YES to NO is difficult for managers. Once uttered, YES will have a magical property of sticking to you. The difficulty involved in walking it back will mean resources, time, money, image, and leave a nasty taste in your mouth for a lengthy period.

Your reputation will change from a Mr. Efficient to Mr. Hopeless in 2 seconds. To say Yes means that you have accepted a proposal to change what already exists to something unknown.
By saying YES without revision, thought, study, and informing all who would be touched by the consequences will create a managerial disaster, which will blow through the organisation.
The damage can manifest itself as a calm shiver to a full-blown hurricane blasting away at all levels of the organisation.
Your Boss will find out, as will all other levels of the management team. Worst of all, your subordinates will lose any respect they have in you. Your image with the employees will be damaged goods.
The Union rep will be banging on the door, or worse your boss' door.

Even if you have a positive reaction to a question, your strategy should always be the negative. Make the noises. Then seek a second opinion from a same level manager or the Boss.
By never giving a positive answer you are buying time, giving you the opportunity to show how reasonable you are. Find out the effects of each element. Analyse. Cost it out. Impacts and time management. Speak to colleagues. Speak to the Boss. Tell him you said NO. Give him your arguments for maintenance of the NO or to change it to a YES.

When the NO is upheld then the dialog stays the same. It's business as usual. You can even speak to the requester of the possible change with a follow up to ensure that the reason for the NO is not workable for x, y, and z reasons.

If I have the OK from upstairs and with the correct analysis and back up the following words sound like an aria by Pavarotti….

'I've been thinking about the negative answer I gave you for the (Budget), (procedure), (deadline), (software change), (Marketing), (Proposal), (Day Off), and after a good look at all the aspects, IT'S A GO. LET 'S DO IT. Good work. '

Give the employee the support he needs to get the job done. Supplies, software, and the time to follow it up. Be aware that people crave recognition. Many people, especially young and hungry employees want recognition more than anything. They will work more hours just for the chance to show their worth as an innovator.

Chapter 3

Strategic Management.

Here is the one shape fits all methodology to motivate your team.
All of your subordinates.
All your children.
Your Boss.
Your Spouse.
Your Kids.
Your Higher Ups

It works.

I have trained commercial managers and Government Managers, and non-profit managers to install and utilise the simple steps associated with Strategic Management.
I implement Strategic Management to encourage the evolution of every participant to a level of expertise, motivation or coaching required to help reach new heights of competence. Each Manager was aware of their exact competence level of motivating and coaching at the start. Everybody has a different profile and the concept ensures that training, promotion, evaluations and forward looking positioning will show all participants that they can immediately understand their level of competence and how to manage others.

Learn these simple methods, and to know application of them to motivate and support your team to ensure maximum effort and results of all concerned.
The applications are simple. It can be explained in 10 minutes to any reasonably intelligent person. Once locked in to the user, it becomes the go to tool to motivate and evaluate the subject and ensure the level of technical competence required.

When giving evaluations to employees there are many biases and assumptions that need to be removed from the process. Honesty is the only way to give an evaluation. If we are not honest, we are not only misrepresenting the work of the subject, but we are misinforming the organisation also. We are cheating the system and the employee may find himself with a promotion, where he may be incapable of completing his mandate, or worse a high flyer that is left behind with a missed opportunity.

Accuracy is the first order of business.

Strategic Management will support the process of evaluation depending on the capacity of the subject. Where does the subject lie in the solution of Strategic Management?

Each subject will have a unique positioning based on the analysis of several functions.

The functions in Strategic Management are:

- Time. Not measured by fixed delays, but by 4 distinct periods of practice and applied growth.
- Management Perception as employees being involved themselves towards a better solution for work.
- Participant Interaction.
- Establishing a level of motivation/coaching to be used over the agreed periods.
- Feedback at every change of period.
- Every task in our lives can be examined and applied to Strategic Management. Work, Playing Golf, Project Management, Playing the Violin, Budget Analysis, Coding…. All followed and managed by the Strategic Manager.

The Time element consists of four distinct periods through which the participant will pass. Each one of these periods asks the manager to see how far the participant has progressed in his travels to achieve his tasks. The four periods are divided into:

- Beginner.
- Intermediate.
- False Expertise.
- Master.

The Beginner, as it implies, represents the participant at the get-go. What knowledge does he bring? What is his orientation to the task at hand? We assume that the beginner has zero competence to the task. Nothing. He is a blank work of art. How do we manage our newbie? There are two measurements we must make with our beginner. One based on Motivation and the other on Expertise.

Motivation is required to learn. Without motivation the required results will not be achieved. The beginner at the start of his travails, in most cases requires no motivation. He wants to learn. He will explore his environment. His interest will be piqued. Catch yourself when you started to play golf, a new job, learning a language learning to paint, everything we do in life has a starting point. We want to do it, however we don't have the expertise to do so.
How do we measure our goals?
How do we reach excellence in our endeavours?
Malcolm Gladwell in The Outliers gave it 10 000 hours then a master you are. I think that this number is a variable. We can't rubber-stamp everyone to the level of 10 000 hours. Some will be 5 000, some will be even less. Most full time employees work 2040 hours per year.

No one will become experts at the same time. We are all working at our pace, but this method makes us observe the pace therefore knowing the measurement, we are capable of observing better than anyone else. When we introduce a new activity, work method, goal, whether personal or work, we are highly motivated and it shows. The technical side may need work.

What is the expertise of the beginner, and how can we measure the level of competence? This is a trick question. We assume that the Beginner has no expertise at the start of the process. We start from a zero competence point.

So at what levels are our two measurements (Motivation and Coaching).

Simply put.....

Motivation at 0 percent.

Instruction at 100 percent.

No motivation? Not needed. The candidate needs none. They need knowledge. They need to know the software. The Procedures. The Budget. The Golf Swing. The Competition. The Products. Marketing. Engineering. School. Badminton. Gym. Diet. Marriage.

They crave knowledge. Their thirst is large. We must quench this thirst with wise words of HOW WE DO IT. This first step of the journey to excellence must be only WHAT makes it all work.

They have no need for motivation. They have brought their own motivation to the table. We have no purpose in increasing their level of motivation, as we probably would be incapable to beat it!

So we leave it alone. Don't mess with the best.

Intermediate.

The participant has been introduced to Strategic Management. He has started his journey to become a knowledgeable member of our team. He has been learning the ins and outs of our activities. HOW to do it. We continue with more HOW. Showing the eccentricities of our expertise.

We are moving forward.

But wait.

What is going on here?

More instruction??

Yes, more instruction.

I know how to do this by now!
Not quite!

I think I have this down pat!
No, you need more practice.

Bump in the road here. At this point where the participant has had the initial introduction, training and coaching we arrive at the next level. The time frame is not important as it is a variable. There are obvious distinctions between nuclear medicine and bar tending, but the principle stays solid.

However in some cases we may encounter a problem. The participant is moving ahead. She has been working diligently due to her motivation. We have been progressively advancing her knowledge. However for her the practice is getting boring. The repetitive part of the activity is becoming long. *I still like it but I want to move faster*. These perceptions are all valid. But the journey is well mapped and we need to achieve all the marks to reach our goals. We need to stay on the road.

The manager's role is to change the mix of motivation and coaching.

Motivation applied at 25% to 50% of time.

Coaching and Instruction at 75% to 50% of time.

Still ensuring that the participant is exposed to supervision at 75%, to 50%, now motivation is applied to the mix.

With advancement the applicant will be able to achieve satisfactory results in all activities.
However there may be resistance to supervisors who correct their work habits. Shortcuts may expose themselves. Laziness may show its ugly

face. Shoddy work may creep in, especially with repetitive work that can be boring.

The manager must ensure that the work is done correctly according to the procedure.

Still give a Pat on the Back. A good word. Encouragement. Recognition. All good. Motivation at a level of around 25% to 50%.

The applicant is still in a period of learning. She still needs coaching and instruction and with time becoming effective at what she does.

False Expertise.

The third segment is the most difficult.

Motivation applied at 100%.

Instruction applied at 0%

At this point the applicant has finished the process of learning the task, activity, project, procedure or finishing.

She can do the job. She has mastered the process. At this level don't go telling her that she made a mistake or try to tell her that her evaluation was less than A1++. When we went through the process described before there is a brief malaise, which must be addressed.

Have you heard this before…? 'Don't tell me how to do my job'; I can do this better than you'; 'I don't need supervised, I know what I'm doing. '

At this level of interaction the applicant may perceive that they have the goods to be unsupervised, as she has learned all that she has to learn about her activities.

Unfortunately this is not the case. The final step is the complete maturity of the applicant.

If we lose her, this is the point where it will happen.

Master.

Motivation applied at 0%

Instruction applied at 0%

By applying each step accordingly the applicant will have followed through each level. There will be 100% of motivation and 100% of knowledge applied to the task at hand by her and not you.

This does not eliminate supervision, but it ensures that the managers tasks will be well planned, organised, directed and controlled.

Any employee or subordinates to you can be analysed easily by using this technique. A simple interview or even chat will give you enough information to map her in the correct level of advancement in Strategic Management. Delivered sincerely with honesty will help her and you to advance the business at hand.

Management Perception implies that the manager must be aware of all the elements at his disposition to correctly analyse where the periods end and begin. The manager must be sold on the use and the function of Strategic Management. This is an essential component.

Chapter 4

Time Management.

How is your time management?
Do you use your time in the most efficient way possible?
Do you watch the clock?
Do you return calls?
Do you procrastinate?

What's the deal with time management?

Let's have a look. How many minutes of the day could you save if you just worked at a level of proficiency? Not at light speed. Not at mule speed. If you are slow on your communications then get faster. Your productivity will go up by bounds. Your bottom line will go up. Sounds dumb. But sometimes we have to dumb things down.

Let's have a look at types of communication within the workplace which you, as a manager, may have contact with in a regular day. There are many means of communication, which are available in today's business environment, which may need a certain level of expertise to successfully navigate all the different forms.

Email: Use two emails. One for work and one for personal use. Never, I mean NEVER use your personal email while you are working. Make your personal emails on your breaks or on your lunch. You are paid to be present and productive. Checking the sports scores, celebrity news, or anything, which is not business, must be eradicated from your attention. You must do this and enjoin your subordinates to do the same.
Insist that personal email is not allowed, from the top to the bottom. There are enough distractions in the day-to-day operations of any business without having to treat employees as 14-year-old children for emailing anyone not related to our work.

Our culture has changed where we seem to have to check emails every 10 seconds for personal reasons. At the office the only important ones are the office emails either incoming or outgoing.

Your family, if they need you urgently, will have your office phone number. Since the early 20th century to maybe 10 years ago we contacted our families at the office. If we had to contact our family urgently, calling the office was good enough. If it were important your manager or you would allow this as normal communications. An email showing a cute puppy or your Aunts' 70th Birthday Party video from last night is not normal communications in a business environment, unless you sell cute puppies.

Make sure that your reporters have a written procedure concerning emails. Your rules about company and private emails have to be explained. Be fair in all things, but be careful of letting the leash go too far. As we say, once permission is given in any field of work, it is one tough cookie to get back. I explain the yes/no problem in this book. No before Yes works. Yes before No is broken.

An interjection of humour should be played when launching such a beast as online practices. Something along the lines of 'Our policy is to uniquely use your business email and keep a record of all strings and messages to be archived under your employee # in the email manager. Please no hockey practice calendars. '

Texting is of the same beast.

Texts: Worse than email. How many texts a day? Time each Text that comes in. Text arrives…Mobile Phone makes an annoying noise……Open Text application……Check who sent the text……..Johnny wants to be friends…….I don't know Johnny…….Send back message……I don't know you…….blah blah blah……..blah blah….ENOUGH!!!

No More. You could make a customer sales call in the same time. You could finish your task whether a client courtesy call or a call to a supplier to get rates reduced, or follow up to a prospect or follow up on the boss's request…..Don't answer non-business messages on your Cell Phone.!!! Take care of this on your break. Don't force the boss to yell. He has a job and one of his responsibilities is to see that you do yours.

Computer Use : Only have programs and software on your work computer, which are authorised by the company. Do not install anything, which could not be explained to your boss if she found it.

Instagram....NO....Facebook.....NO ..CASINO/GAMBLING ....NO.........SHOPPING ......NO....YOUTUBE......NO..... Porno....Indeed....Whatever the next big thing is...

Unless of course it is part of your job.

All of the workforce need to use online resources. It's unusual in this era not to see the vast majority of staff work directly on the web all day long. Your job is to use those resources to complete the work being done. Call centers, sales departments, warranty houses, insurance claims, banks, any large enterprise has their own web, database, and business software, which is used by ALL of their employees, managers included. Your point towards subordinates is to insist the unique usage of in-house needs. Leave all your personal online navigation for home, lunch, and on breaks. The non-authorised use of these assets, of course, should not be open for time wasting, added expenses, slow down on productivity, mistakes, and an unhealthy trend towards laziness. You must be aware of the use of computers on your watch. Be hard on abuse. If an employee or manager continues this behaviour bring them in for a quiet chat to resolve their behaviour.

Keep your computer tidy. Have a clean screen. Have the icons well defined, and organised. Make it easy to navigate so that if someone has to take your place for the day they will be able to follow your work easily and carry on with the productive activities of the day. You should be able to go to a colleagues' computer and find your way around it with complete ease. Any group working within the same group should be capable to orient her with great ease into the position.

Your Day

Get up in the morning. Don't get out of bed at the last minute possible.

If, like the vast majority of people, you have a regular job with regular hours, you will benefit from being early for everything. Getting up and about at early days will give you the space required to be on your toes and up for anything.

I have frequently started my day at four a.m. Some of my activities are;

- Make a killer spreadsheet on Excel
- Make sense of the report on our clients proposition
- Plan my recruiting calls for the day
- Finish off employee evaluations needing to be delivered

I say try this. Not everyone can do this. Try it though. You will bet used to it rapidly and you will benefit.

Being early in everything will denote you as a heavyweight in the office.

Do your toughest job first. Always start with the most difficult task you have perceived among all your to do list on the day. Make this the first order of business. It could look like this;

- Call XYZ Sprockets to cancel the order
- Inform Candidate #4 that their application has been declined
- Speak to the Boss to inform him that the software developer has backed up production of the app and it wont be ready for launch

Never keep the horrible news to yourself. Never be afraid to give anyone the bad news. If you can't give the bad news, then you are not a manager. Anyone can give the good news. Easy. Share price is up. Easy. Projections are on the mark. Easy. Staff costs are down. Easy. Buy a monkey to give the good news. Put your pants on to give the bad news.

If you don't get the tough calls, emails, memos done early in the day, your procrastinations will crawl out of the woodwork and cause all kind of trouble. It is the easiest way to trip up your day. Miss an early chance to fix the difficult files will leave you with a problem. The day will get longer. Nine a.m. will quickly become eleven a.m. which will become one p.m. Lunch. Meeting. Caught by Mr. Talk-a-lot. Meeting. All of a sudden you will have no tough files completed. They must be done early. It will be a lead weight around your neck all day. It will drag you slowly down.

The job not done the day before will still be there when return to the office and there will be an additional slate of problems that need prioritised for tomorrow morning. What will happen in the end is that your boss will see what's going on and will pass the job over to someone else. Don't think that you won't be called out. You will be. So be secure. Do it NOW. Your colleagues and the Boss need to know.

Arrive at work earlier than your employees. Your employees measure you every day as to your work practices. It's tough to give a reprimand for tardiness when you show up for work after them. Credibility loss.

Get going as soon as possible. Why are we here? We are here to do our jobs.

Good.

Tasks and events show up every day. Some are complicated. Some are simple yes/no questions. They are all important for one or more members of your organisation or even other organisations. Send them to the right person immediately.

Some tasks require contributions from other experts, higher ups, lower downs, equal levels, department heads, assistants heads, general managers, shareholders, owners. Everyone in an organisation has tasks either sourced by them or delegated by managers and all tasks are important for all people in the organisation. They must be respected as such.

When you have a task. JUST DO IT. Do not waste time. Wasting time is lost time. You will never get it back. Time is the only element that we have which we can never replace. So why do we waste time. Procrastination's nomenclature should be changed to *You are wasting away your life.*

If you have a report to do that is due next week, try to do it now.
If you have an evaluation due in two weeks, try to do it now.
If that pricing structure is due tomorrow, try to do it now.
If that budget is due in three months, try to do it now.

Don't worry about the date. If your tasks are completed as arrived and you are always up to date then you will be a heavyweight.

Don't make excuses when you miss deadlines. The file will be noticed as being late. Your boss will not be happy. Don't be late. However, if you *are* going to be late, let the receiver of the information know as soon as possible, or ask for help. Telling someone that you will be late in 10 minutes does not give you points. Telling someone that you will be late the day before is OK. When we are aware of tardiness and share it early, there is less of an annoyance factor at play. It is easier to move a meeting the day before than just before.

Don't let employees who are supposed to be doing tasks, to open their computers on news sites or email unless they need the information, which regard our business. If you catch someone doing this on a regular basis, task him to provide you with a report on how much the organisation loses by inappropriate usage of company internet resources in dollar amounts. Have him do séances with all employees to show the losses acquired by the company through this practice. This will certainly have an impact on the employee. Congratulate the employee on his excellent work publicly. We are all winners. The company for reducing costs, the employee for his excellent work, you the manager, for closing a cash whirlpool on the company dime.

Do not work all day, all evening, all night. You are not Superman. If you are working 10, 12, 14 hours a day then you are not doing your job. You are doing 2 peoples jobs.

Do not take work home with you. If you cannot complete your work within the time allotted then your department is under staffed at your level, or you are incapable of delegating work by asking for more staff. Don't be shy to ask as you the need the personnel, just be sure that you have the proof available.

Go home when the bell goes. Do not bring work home with you. You are not paid for this work. In some cases we are required to work a few hours later. New software, new office opening, facility upgrades. These tend to be exceptional circumstances. I worked to open a new casino in a high level market, over a period of three months with a billion dollar budget. The time frame was very tight. My longest stretch was 90 days and a workday of between 10 and 14 hours. This is extreme and I don't recommend it for anyone.

However, the emotional rush of completion on time and on budget was exhilarating. But I would think twice before repeating the exercise.

Taking one day's problems and ploughing them over to the next day is problematic and discouraging. If you are really stuck and the clock is flying fast to 5 pm then what the hell! Ask colleagues if they have a fix. If so, copy it. Ask the question. See if you have a fit, then integrate it.

If your boss sticks around the office for 12-hour days, don't fall into the flytrap of following his example. If the President of the company does the same, and he asks you to stick around, you must weigh the answer very carefully. Once in, it is nearly impossible to get out. Do not become a member of this club unless your evaluation of the situation will reward you with all kinds of goodies.

You are a heavyweight between 9 and 5. 12-hour days will soon turn you into a lightweight. Not because you can't do your job, but because you have agreed to join in a prolonged day for show. Look at us! We are the guys who know our business, because we're here all day, all night.

Once home enjoy your family.

DO NOT TAKE DRUGS…DO NOT SHOW UP AT WORK WITH A HANGOVER…NEVER DRINK ALCOHOL AT WORK. It's that simple. If you do your boss will know, your business partners will know, your customers will know. Enough said.

Getting to work

Do not be late for work.

Never, ever for any reason whatsoever, be late for work. It is the one element, which you must respect at all times without any excuse. Never. No Excuse. Never.

Being lost is not good

Do you have employees or bosses or anyone in your office that you can never find?
Missing in Action. Your secretary, your colleagues, your subordinates, your boss should know at all times where you are during the working day. As you should know where the boss is, so you should know where the secretary is or your administrator.

Stepping out to get some air? Tell your Secretary. Going down to the plant floor? Tell the admin. Showing a new partner around our retail spaces? Tell your Secretary. Out of town? On vacation? Let those who need to be aware of your whereabouts know where you are. Always!

Only send your calls to your Secretary or the call center when you must deal with a situation that requires your complete attention. This could be an employee evaluation. During a union negotiation. Client negotiation. Asking for money. Use your good judgement. If you have someone in your office from an outside source you should send your calls to your secretary, or the call center. When the face to face has ended then return those calls immediately. How do you like it when you leave a message and there is no call back for hours, days, weeks or even months? Do unto others as you would have them do unto you. Call back promptly.

When you have a face to face in your office, never have a disruption. No phone calls, no text, not checking your email squinting at the computer, no interruptions. Your demeanour is towards your guest. Show respect. If you show interest to any distraction while in company of a visitor you are showing them that all the interruptions are more important than them. Not a nice feeling.

At your office, don't have the secretary answer your calls. You should answer them. I find it ridiculous to have the secretary answer the phone, 'Mr. Dickson's Office ', 'Hello, Is Mr. Dickson in?', 'Yes, shall I direct your call?', 'Yes, please.', 'What's the name?'. Mr. Waiting-on-the-phone!'

Why is it so difficult to pick up your own phone call!!
Rather than having a secretary to vet your calls, just answer the call. It's so easy. 'No.', 'Yes.' 'Not now.' 'We have this already in place.' 'Please stop calling me, I will call you if I have a need.' 'Thank you, but I have this already.'

Don't have your secretary call someone you want to talk to. Call her yourself. By doing this you make the secretary more productive. Instead of having 2 people trying to find someone, I call them, I get a hold of them, I leave a message, and I get the call back. Instead of creating a wall between yourself and the world, take your responsibilities to task. Be reachable. Reachable is talk able. Communications are improved.

When looking for information, advice, or have a problem and you phone the resource, and the secretary answers, ask for the person you want to talk to. If the secretary or telephonist wants to take a message just say your name and phone number and that it is urgent. That is all, nothing else. If they ask the reason of the call repeat that it is urgent. Then hang-up. We do this because there is a danger that they will ask why you called. Now you will be in a situation to describe what you require from the wrong person. The secretary will not know what needs to be done, so why waste your time? Time Wasting. Useless practice. Just get the call back. How many people need to know our business to get through to the person I want to talk to? It is not rude. It is good time management.

Imagine the extra time that you can use in productive activities instead of waiting for your secretary to tell you that your target is in a meeting and will she leave a message and the tell her what to leave......Blah, Blah, Blah...you get the picture?

Chapter 5

Office and Visibility

If you have your own office and don't share it with a co-worker, be aware of the layout, furniture, computer, lighting, windows and visibility.

The door is open at all times except when;
I am meeting one or more persons.
I am on a confidential call.
I am working with confidential documents on my desk.
I am out of the office.

The door should have a glass partition, so that anyone passing can see that I am at my workplace.
The furniture should include one desk with several drawers. I prefer wood instead of chrome and aluminum, but there you are!

A lamp on the desk.
A laptop computer with a hub to make it a desktop.
A hands free telephone.
A filing cabinet.
Two chairs in front of the desk.
Two rows of lighting above the desk.

Your briefcase should be on one of the chairs.
On the other chair you should have your coat.
They should stay there all day unless you have outside visitors or you have an agreed meeting on your calendar.
If there are more than two visitors then take the meeting to the Board Room.

When you have a visitor from either inside or outside the organisation prepare your office. This could be a possible recruit, salesperson, employee, IT, HR or any possible combination that has an appointment. Preparation is organised as this;

- No papers on the desk
- Lights on
- Shutters closed except for one
- Telephone forwarded

When the guest arrives you will be looking outside the window with your back to the door and your hands clasped behind your back. The visitor will knock at the door, which is half open. You will turn and invite them in and shake their hand and welcome them by name.
A firm handshake. A wimpy, loose handshake has no value and does not convey confidence. The handshake has to have several elements to be effective and leave the recipient impressed and trusting.

- Look her in the eyes and smile
- Hold the hand firmly but not a tight squeeze
- One firm quick shake
- Say, 'Delighted to see you today, Ms Jones.'
- Let go

This simple preparation and welcome will open communication in a trustworthy atmosphere. Cordial and polite behaviour will generate intelligent conversation. Do not make conversation filled with assumptions with your interlocker, like, 'Love the Redskins', or 'Can you believe that they elected that idiot?' You will only lose any credibility that you have already established.

In all conversations with suppliers, employees, bosses, customers at a meeting with one or many or any one do not under any circumstances:

- Ask or admit your political leanings
- Ask or admit your sexual orientation
- Check your phone
- Tell edgy jokes
- Start doodling
- Take calls
- YAWN…………..
- Scratch your nose or other body parts
- Promise you will commit. No before Yes always

On the other hand these are required for a successful meeting;

- Remember her name
- Pay attention with eye contact
- Ask intelligent, relevant questions
- Have courage to ask the difficult question
- Listen
- Be early
- Take notes
- Agree to follow-up
- Make sure all parties are on the same map for any deliverables and dates

Chapter 6

Distractions

We have 8 hours a day to complete our work. Therefore we have to guard ourselves from the elements that can reduce these hours by wasting our time and therefore the enterprise's.

One of these elements is the Big Gob that pokes her head around the door every now and again. Big Gob can destroy your day. Big Gob can take you from having a run of productivity to a Titanic event. They must be avoided like the plague.

Knock on the door. Head pops around. 'Hello' says Big Gob. 'What about those Red Sox?' What about Trump this week? Markets going wild, eh? How was your weekend? Did you see the new Starbucks across the street?

You must discourage the beast as quickly as possible. Your day will be shot if you don't defuse her immediately. How long do you think it takes to lose Big Gob? You have to pick her up and kick her out of your office.

Of course this wouldn't be politically correct. So we use our heads. First of all the 2 chairs in front of my desk are there just for Big Gob. She can't sit down. There is briefcase on one seat and a coat on the other. This will make her uncomfortable. She will look around for a place to sit, but can't. She is in a tough position because she is looking for a conversation about nothing and I am trying to get her out the smoothest way possible. If she wanted a business conversation I would be all ears, but Big Gob wants a conversation every day with everybody. She has to go. To get her out of the office you have to get out of you chair, go to her, hold her elbow and lead her to your door, telling her that you have a very important call to make right now. She will go. If she is your report, speak to her about this behaviour quickly.

It can destroy productivity. Imagine if she grabbed 5 managers a day for even 5 minutes. 25 minutes a day, 125 minutes a week, which equals around 14 days a year of nonsense. Unacceptable waste of productivity for gobbledygook.

Big Gob behaviour has to be eradicated.

Big Gob changes when she is not chasing you down. While she wears the Big Gob hat with you she changes her hat for her fellow employees. Her compatriots in the office know her as the Fish Wife. She can't stop talking about nothing and pulling everyone away from what they should be doing.

Fish Wife likes to tell everyone about her life. Her yoga class, her hairdresser, The Voice, Dancing with the Stars, the traffic, the coffee, and the weather. It doesn't stop. She knows everything about everything, or she knows who does.

Fish Wife has 4 kids who play Hockey or Football and we hear every play of the weekend on a Monday morning. We know what she eats for Breakfast, lunch and dinner.

She calls her husband hubby and he calls his wife, 'Her Indoors'.

Fish Wife has to be talked to. There are ways to operate and remove this blockage in the organisation.

To remove the Fish Wife, we have to remove her fixation on all things not associated with work. People tend to act like Fish Wife when they are bored at work or have too much time on their hands, therefore give her a tougher job.

Train her to be more polyvalent within the organisation. Make her busier than she is. If you don't make her more occupied and quieter she can disrupt your operations. Snip, snip. Use the Math again. How much time does she swallow from everyone else?

End the madness. Be smart about it. She has become this way through having her co-workers and, more importantly her supervisors, allow this nonsense to continue. We all like a laugh and even an interaction, but not at the cost of productivity. Are we a social club, a gossip chat show on TV or are we a business fighting the competition at our best fighting weight?

Looking at these elements that are a part of every organisations make-up we have to make a decision where the elimination of Yak is approved. Lunch and breaks. OK. Working hours NO. Verboten. Ne pas Permis. Culture this in and you will save time and money, which will look like a new revenue flow.

One of the killers of productivity in any business is the Barrack-Room Lawyer. In some quarters they are called the Backstabbers. Every organisation has at least one in every level of the hierarchy.

You know them. You've seen them every day. They know more than everyone else. They have opinions on every aspect of the organisation. Sales, Marketing, Software, HR, Management, Shareholders, everything that touches the business. They do their jobs for the most part, but they can poison other employees. They are easy to spot. They will come into your office with a 2-knock tap on the door and a head pops in asking if you have a minute.

BRL has an opinion that he has to share with you. He is more dangerous than Big Gob and Fish Wife together. This animal doesn't just yak on about trivial nonsense. This monster has an opinion on every facet of the operation. He will tell you like it is. He has never been wrong about anything and likes to let everyone know.

A beast of the jungle. His proclamations are half-baked, increasingly disruptive and require to be sliced out of the business. If not then things will only get worse. The longer his tenure as BRL the more vitriol he will spout. Do not tolerate the BRL in any way. Putting him out of his misery will only improve the atmosphere, culture and productivity of every aspect of your business. Beware the BRL.

If you can't surgically remove him, then you may have to be cruel to be kind. Be brutal. The BRL will also stab you in the back when he has the chance. He will diss your boss and his boss and the receptionist and Charlie in HR and Betty in Sales and Tasso in IT. Be sure that he will diss you when you are not around. He will take every opportunity presented to him to take you down just as vocally as he has anyone else.

From the President of the company to the cleaning crew. His disdain may come from many sources. Huge Beef from not being promoted fast enough. His project for the widgets was refused. You piped him for the last promotion. The BRL is furious with his lot. He thinks he should be the CEO, CFO, CTO, DG, Chairman, Chief Bottle Washer, and the guy who calls the shots for everything that happens within the organisation. STAB, STAB, STAB.

People who are highly intelligent, but who are lazy have tendencies to join the league of BRL. They are smart. They nail everything. They know everything. If you equated their scholarly achievements they would be one of the smartest people in the firm.

A 1st from a major university. Published papers on several subjects. Profound. Well spoken. But lazy. They don't recognise their own mal. They know how smart they are and they think they are the smartest in the room. In some cases they are. But they only want to hear the sound of their name which they adore They love to show anyone who wants, or doesn't want to hear how, if he was the Big Kahuna, how this would be different.

'Chalmers should be on IT duty. The last round of financing should have been at 2.75%, they don't know what they are doing. The menu at the caff is gross. The CEO spends too much time at the lawyers. The Cleaning Crew should use product X. If only I was on the board.'

He wants to hear you say that he is the best and he should be running the whole shebang. And if you don't you will be next on the diss list next time he finds a victim. The BRL needs to be moved quickly to the door, or placed in a position where he can do the least damage to the business at hand. If he continues then a move out the door is only solution. When the day arrives that his nonsense has been finally recognised by the organization then there must be a waterproof document signed which ensures his silence.

Critics

Standing by the coffee machine Claudia and Annette are having a good old natter about how Germaine really duffed the last budget. How many of you have been involved in a conversation like this?

I am convinced that around Zero AD, when Hadrians' Wall was erected between the countries of Scotland and England, there were two Roman Centurions talking together when they were guarding the Wall. Claudius said to Antonius, ' Germanicus really duffed the last budget.' 'Who's idea was it to build a wall and guard it here? That Hadrian doesn't know what he's doing!'

Lots of times this nattering is pointed directly at the boss, or another department boss or the new girl. As long as they don't mention each other. I'm pretty sure that any reader will be aware.

If someone is capable to talk bad about someone to you, then she will be capable to doing the exact same behaviour towards you. This action helps the actors feel good about them selves. They are too busy dissing out the subject to realise they are being talked about themselves somewhere in the building.

We all have a good memory of our feathers in the cap. Introduction of new process, receivables down to 5% per month from 10%. You will never forget these great victories that have been accomplished using your sweat.

Unfortunately your recollection for these great victories that light up your life will not be shared. Even Bosses can use the great, 'What have you done for me lately?' line. You can only ride the winning horse once at a time.

To maintain your lap of honour, you must keep on winning. People can be easily irritated by your success. It's human nature. We tend to forget our failures, never our successes. It feels so good to succeed that we forget the bad. Be aware of the duds. That goes for everyone. So be attentive to all around you.

Give a pat on the back to those who deserve it. Even if it seems that a competitor of yours hits a home run, congrats are in order. When you hit the home run, don't expect the same reaction. Sometimes it is difficult to pat someone when there's been a lot of chitchat at the water fountain.

Chapter 7

Employees

As a manager you have a responsibility towards the owners of the business. Whether it is a sole ownership, partnership, CEO, Shareholders, and Non-Profit Board of Directors. The guidance given to the managers of the entity must apply the directions given to ensure the success of the objectives.

Most entities have a profit objective. Once we strip away all the fluff about good governance, neighbourhood partners, sponsorships, when we reach the year end the first order of business is sales minus costs = the profit. Maximise sales, Minimise Costs.

As a manager you may be an expert in your domain, which is needed because of complex activities. A good example of this would be HR, another could be Finance. At these levels the requirements are usually a degree in the function they occupy. Less and less specialisation as we move up the organisational ladder is required. The higher we go the more polyvalent your repertoire becomes.

It is rare that you find a head of department in Engineering who has no such degree. Quantity Surveyors are another good example where specialists are required as not many people understand what they do. I had a good friend who worked as a QS. He told me that he walked around building sites drinking tea looking busy two days out of three.

When we prove ourselves as having the right stuff to occupy the High Sierra of a Boardroom, or be the Head of the Head Department, or of Director of Administration, then we can suddenly find ourselves with a ticket to high managing.

All of a sudden, you find yourself as the Director of Administration, being promoted from the post of Director of Buildings. You may now find yourself the boss of the Director of Admin, of HR, of Finance, of IT, of Call Centers, of Legal Affairs.

Five or six reporters are usual in organisations, more than that tends to overload. If you are good, you can ask for more. If you are bad then your boss might take some back.

Managers look at departments in organisations as badges of honour or as badges of penitentiaries. In every organisation certain departments are considered gold plated and are coveted. Another will draw an 'Oh No' reaction from the Director awarded a dud department. It could be any one.

I worked in an organisation where Administration was feared as a department. Many a good man and woman tried to crack it, but failure was high. Disasters were common. Elevators broken down. Cleaning not done. Doors locked. Invoices not taken care of. Unionised staff restless. Weak managers creating a department that was feared by potential bosses.

However, when a strong manager took the reins the department became the strongest in the house. He was Fast, Fair, Firm, Focused and occasionally Funny. This Heavyweight could go in anywhere and manage from day one. His secret was that he managed the department like he had managed every job he was given. He Planned, Organised, Directed and Controlled his activities. He had a well-founded understanding of people.

Management is needed in any environment requiring structure and continuity and when applied correctly with an application of reasonably consistent rules and regulations, it works. Problems are resolved quickly. Communications are integrated not only with official channels but also with informal channels. These two channels should be used together to meet management objectives. Understanding them and using them properly can ensure two sources underlining the same message. Beefs are allowed to be open not shunned. All staff will receive the same information from both sources thereby reinforcing the message. Every morning and every afternoon we would say, 'that's another file completed.'
And so it goes.

The more problem files are attacked and resolved, there is more acceleration to the resolution of all the problems. They will never be totally fixed. There will always be new problems requiring resolution. If that didn't happen then managers would become extinct.

How do you recognise a competent manager just by observation?

When I first enter a manager's office I have a good look around the environment that he works in. As I mentioned before the manager's office should be pretty sparse relating to work. I look for tomes on management lining a shelf. The library stands as proof of the manager's education and prowess in his field. Mmm.

Ask him the last management book that he read. You might be surprised. If he has a copy of this book then kudos. Do you need 20, 30, 40 management books adorning your office? Do you think that if he was reading these books was he being effective at his profession and would he have time to work?

Books are a sign of pride. Is he really going to read one of them if he has a problem? The books are there to strut up his ego by trying to impress reporters who are summoned to his office. Don't let the books impress you. They are a common sign of a manager who is insecure of his métier.

How is his desk stacked? How many papers are sitting on his desk? How deep is it? Are there any confidential files open on the desk? A clean desk shows competence. If invited to the office, the manager who respects himself and their reporter will have a clean desk. The only paper on the desk will be the project at hand or none at all. Anything else is sloppy. It shows a lack of respect to the visitor and his work.

I feel better and more comfortable meeting when the office is impeccable. I prepare for the visit five minutes before it is to start. I get acquainted with the latest report and the faits saillents of the file. With one minute before the meeting I stand and wait at the door. I am ready. I am never late for meetings. I don't expect anyone else to be late. My guest arrives to a waiting manager in a clean environment and we are down to the subject at hand.

Meetings should be recorded by minutes. Minutes are a requirement. If there is no file to peruse, always have a clean sheet of A4 on the desk. Quickly make minutes of what you have to do and what she has to do. Date the required items for time verification or finish date. Cost projections and project deadlines.

Other interventions, either by committees or higher ups. Send a cc to all persons who may be affected by the meeting. If it is a meeting, which touches HR, cc your HR liaison. Touches software, cc IT management. Touches procedure change, cc Operations. Enter the dates agreed to your outlook calendar or your usual calendar/to-do. There is not much these tools cannot do to remind you on a daily basis to manage your time from an outlook to project, in today's environment you must have this.

There is nothing worse for a manager than missing a meeting, missing a deadline, missing a report, missing a technology, missing anything just by dozing at the switch. One miss will be tough for you, two will be all over the organisation, three and you will be an ex-manager. Make sure that you do it. Meetings are when business is done, Record, Send, and Review your deadlines.

If you have a subordinate who wants to see you in your office out of the blue, the inclination may be to find out what she wants first and preparing yourself. I do not recommend this. Get her up to the office right away. Meet with her and take care of business. It may be an ask for a raffle ticket at her daughters skating club. It may be a request for extra time off, a complaint about a supervisor, or she may have found a way to save the company money. By meeting quickly, you save time. You have moved on.

Meet every single person in the organisation under you. Factory workers. Accountants, Senior Managers, Dishwashers, Vehicle drivers. Anyone who reports to someone who reports to you. Say Hello. How are you doing today? Thanks for your contribution. Thank you. It takes 10 seconds on average. Do this every opportunity.

Your job as a manager covers many facets. You are there to be the guy or the gal who can call the shots to move the business forward. Your actual activities as a manager will probably be integrated into a document called the Job Description. I have never seen a Job Description, which was held to account by its contents.

I have seen managers fired concerning activities that they were asked to complete outside their Job Description. Managers, unless they are a part of a management brotherhood, generally have little or no protection against what could be considered an incident not to the liking of the higher ups.

Managers need their work. They need their name. If they have a good managerial profile, to go quietly is the only way in the majority of cases. A fight with lawyers will not help when you interview for a managerial post elsewhere. Heads down, and carry on. If the amount you request as compensation is not high enough for example to finance an early retirement or a start a new business then challenge it. However, lawyers tend to be expensive and if the case stretches out over the months and years these costs certainly become onerous.

HR and the Higher Ups, probably to two levels under them to whom they report, will have elaborated Job Descriptions. Managers write these and also interview for evaluations on same two levels. Fluffy vocabulary should be avoided. The language in the Job Description should be clear, concise, short, and to the point. 'Plan, Organise, Direct and Control all activities in the operations of product x.' 'Ensure the submission of the yearly budget before the 1st April every year.' 'Ensure sales of 10m$ by the 3rd quarter.'

The Job Description should not use washy, washy guesswork for your guidance. I have seen some doozies.
'Keep the employees happy.'
'Organise the social committee for the golf tournament.'
Arrrrrrgggghhhhh.

There are 2 Job Descriptions. One is the Job Description, which is posted either internally or externally. Jobs are advertised everywhere from employment websites to local government offices to newspapers.
The other Job Description is the actual one that is used as an evaluation tool by the manager and HR. There may be some surprises in these documents, which will elaborate activities outside the original brief. Not much you can do about this. Head down and get on with it. They would never hire you if there was any doubt as to your capacity to do the job.

When evaluations get embedded into the company then it becomes a much larger element than the organisation needs.
It becomes;

- Related to any pay increase.
- Related to any possibility of promotion or swapping levels.
- Training required.
- Takes an incredible amount of time to manage.
- Encourages fear among personnel.
- Evaluators boosting markings to boost their evaluation.
- Busy managers will know their staff and evaluate accordingly.

Read your companies Job Description and then the Job Evaluation papers. Is there a difference between the two? Would you as a manager understand exactly what you are evaluating? I wonder.

The Evaluation and Description will always have discrepancies. Some of the items and activates will almost certainly cross over to other evaluations and descriptions.

- Plan, Organise, Direct and Control all activities of Department X.
- Direct and Control the operations of Department X.
- Anticipate the Planning and Direction for the following fiscal year before Q3 of Department X.

You get the picture.

Chapter 9

Hiring

Every company has its own procedure when hiring. It usually involves the manager one or two levels up, a rep from HR and another manager of a senior department.

The parties will draw up a list of questions and the required answers decided. Some questions are weighted to ask for a more detailed answer and a required answer. Some questions are very commonly used in the interview.

The manager will fire relevant questions about the actual work of the department. The HR will ask generic questions on employee management. The senior manager will ask general management questions.

'What is the most important thing you can give your staff?'
Short answer, my time.

'In what situation would you call your immediate supervisor?'
Short answer, at any time anything unusual happens or out with the parameters of the work.

'What percentage of your work time would be utilised for Planning?'
Short answer 60%.

How would you direct an employee who wasn't communicating enough with you?
Answer,' I would tell her that if she thinks I should know, then that becomes a must. She must call me. If it is not serious, I will tell her thank you for the call. If it is serious I will say to her, thank you for the call. Never tell an employee that her call was not relevant. If an employee calls which is not relevant, never tell the employee. The fact that the employee called shows the line of communication is open.

What do you on a daily basis? Short answer. Innovate.
If you are not innovating on a daily basis you are not doing your job as a manager.
Innovation is good for existing products, operations, budgets, employees, and managers, everything that touches the organisation. People and things will be touched by innovation. We are brought to the organisation, not to keep the status quo, but to move everything forward and upward with our vision and collaboration.

Tricky question. 'As a manager you may be asked to work extra hours. What is your feeling on this?' No short answer. Tough call. Are they looking for a no problem, I'm there, or an, I can't do this? Middle up the answer. 'I am always available if my work load needs it, but I keep my desk clean.'

If you are interviewing at an organisation and have not done your homework, you could be cooked. You have to know a little about the culture at the organisation. Then you would have the answer. Do

There is a new track in North America, where IT companies are opening up doors when it comes to work hours. Google, in some campuses have unlimited vacation. This is due to the hours required to complete their work eats up traditional work time. The compensation is the unlimited vacation. The landscape is changing.

Banks at weekends. Schools opening earlier. Car Dealerships at weekends. Good or bad? We will see in the next few decades. A lot of people are going to be out of work. Driverless trucks and cars. Maybe pilotless planes and cargo ships. Retail employees.

During interviews you shouldn't talk too much. The candidate is not there to learn all about your history or your latest project failure. He is there to talk about himself.

I completed this culture change in short thrift……
Q. When and How did you do this?

I turned a shotgun clause that netted the company 5m$.
Q. Please run through the process you used.

43

All candidates must be evaluated based on the requirements of making the company better, more profitable and cost saving. You cannot look at gender, colour, sexual orientation, and physically handicapped candidates and say no thank you. You must hire the best candidate, or if you didn't find her, try again.

If you have a candidate that has shown promise elsewhere and has proved himself in the past; 2 promotions in the past 4 years; 2 papers published and peer reviewed; concrete results in the domain he wants to work in. Winner.

Don't take a chance on an underachieved recruit. If you see missing experiences in the resume or detect lacunes in her answers then mark the resume No. Always make a follow up call to the candidate to decline or accept her. HR should take care of the boarding business and orientation to the company.

If she doesn't show up. Call her and ask why. Then leave her file in HR with a 'do not hire' note.

When hiring you have to try your utmost to sign up the winner. Whether you are hiring inside or outside your choice will have a direct win or lose for the organisation. The winner will be your woman. You will have chosen the next manager. Your choice will certainly be a disappointment for several people who have been waiting on the sidelines, but don't make the cut. There will be hurt souls all around.

Reporters who have reached their potential or those who believe that they have the attributes to be on the express train to higher management but are not picked can be mad, more than disappointed, and rebellious.

The evaluation process that you use should always follow the firm and fair route.
Be firm. Don't hide the weaknesses of the candidate with kind words or insincere platitudes.

Be fair. Always keep your reporters aware of their missing skills. If they are up for the job, place them in the line up. If not tell them. Do not make the mistake of saying next time you might have it. All you are doing is setting her up for a future disappointment down the road.

Maintaining hope for people to be a higher up when you know that person has reached their full potential requires a delicate but realistic conversation being Fair and Firm. Tell them that a move to another department or division would increase their chances of a promotion. Try to make this happen as quickly as possible. You and the employee will be happier. When employees reach this ceiling of their capacities, the next step is a burn out.

The burned comes in all shapes and sizes.

New recruits who turn out to be duds.

Experienced staffs can and do become duds overnight on occasion. They lose the track of the business and can't get back on. When this happens we need to slice with the scalpel and move them out.

This behaviour is common with intelligent, lazy people. They are smart enough to understand the organisation, but think they are smarter than every one else, which mostly they are. With a lazy trait the work can be tedious for very smart people. They drift as they consider the work boring and in the worst scenario she becomes a Barrack Room Lawyer. Move them out. How do you move them out?

First of all we have to identify why the candidate is there in the first place. Previous evaluations or appraisals will show over the years a reasonably good history. I often twin the evaluation with one that I have asked the person to prepare. By having an auto-evaluation we will pinpoint any wide gulf between the realities of their performance. Ask why such a discrepancy should exist.
Managers who have reached the zenith of their abilities cannot be promoted. Reaching the extent of their capacity means that he can't move any further. The result could be disastrous for the organisation.

Making the call for promotion in this case implies that you are at ease with incompetence at a managerial level. This will become your problem in the future. You will be accountable for the promotion of a mistake. These decisions will also define your judgement to the higher ups.

Move to another sector. Tell him that he has reached the top. If he wants to move up then maybe go back to school, get another diploma and start looking. This can be devastating for someone. We need to encourage him, help him to adapt and find another opportunity,

Do not take over a promotion decision if the process has already commenced. This goes for any project, report, budget, IT changes, whatever was on the plate of someone else. Only in the case of a serious illness, or an impossible circumstance should you pick up the possible disaster of another.

As a young manager I took the reins of a competition for a mid manager to run an operations department. There was already a round of candidates, CV's had been collected and the number of candidates was high.
The manager in charge of the competition after a week of no activity, bailed out citing that she felt insecure to call the shots. I was asked by my superior to take care of the file. Being young and keen I gladly accepted the file and got to work.

Out of 20 candidates there were 10 who were already working as interim managers at the same level as the competition. There were several who were considered competent and others who were possibly borderline and some who were considered too early in their development.
To reduce the competition I created an exam based on managerial policies and security common sense to avoid pilfering.

This was a cash handling business that had an ingrained paranoia over possible theft. I considered the exam a filter to move the smarter ones ahead and those who needed coaching would place themselves for the future.

The previous manager had told a potential candidate that she would be a shoe-in. I was unaware of this. The shoe-in came bottom of the contest. No idea. Missed every danger signal. The candidates were met and I gave the feedback. I told the shoe-in that she would not be moving forward. It took me several weeks to resolve this.
She brought in HR, my boss, the original owner of the file, and an external attorney. My decision was upheld.
However, this took many hours of explanation to many parties.

Instead of completing the file in short thrift, questions were asked about techniques and validations of process and were found squeaky clean.
I learned my lesson.

Do Not take a file that already has been started by another unless;

- Don't say Yes, before a No
- Take time to know the whole file before agreeing
- If you are taking over a project from a weak manager. Refuse, unless you have your superior give you the OK to reset the file from the start.

Do not promise jobs to individuals. Sure you will feel good telling someone that you have been grooming for a promotion, who has shown loyalty, good work, commitment and that she is next in line.
Even if that person is the only candidate possible, and there are no other options available don't let it happen. Leave it open and find a replacement quickly.

There must be a competition for the post.
If not there will be rumours of a fix. Organise the protocol. Advertise the post. Ask for CV's. Call all respondents.

Those that are missing qualifications are refused. Meet the candidates. Meet them a second time if required. By telling your favourite that she is a shoe in is a recipe for disaster.

First of all, you will not be interviewing a management post on your own. There will be at least one rep from HR, a senior manager from another department and your immediate supervisor. If they all agree to a different candidate, what is the outcome? You will have lost the confidence of your employee. The word will get out that Sahara didn't get the post, and Sahara will become a problem and the office will be affected.

Leave people with reasonable hopes, but not certificated promises. Your job is to ensure that the facts are in on competence. You can try and sell your employee during the deliberation process, but if your seniors are not on line with you, you may lose the discussion.

Now you are in trouble by being too open, and miscalculating your capacity to push pre-emptive decisions through. This is dangerous all round.

You will deceive your candidate and the perception among the staff will be that you manipulate decisions.

New Recruits landing a dull Boss.

First day on the job. Exciting? Of course. Who is the Boss? Unfortunately the Boss will probably be dull at best. Incompetent at worst. This is your lot. New hires starting at the low ranks will not be working directly for the best managers in the Company.

The reasoning is quite simple. The best Bosses have already moved on. The higher ups are where the better Bosses are when you arrive. The ones who will be directing are either newbies themselves or have reached their own level of incompetence and cannot rise any further.

People move forward and upward based on their performance in the Company. Sales increased/Costs decreased.

Your PH.D in Nuclear Optics isn't going to impress Mr. Stuckinarut.

He has been left behind while his colleagues moved on. You have Mr. Stuckinarut to work with.

In this case you will have to shine over the dullness. Work hard. Produce papers showing revenue generation and cost reductions. Be Polite. Ask for extra work. Be on time. Keep the Boss up to speed.

If the Boss is dull and shows little interest in helping you move up, go looking for another one. Do your best, then some. The weeks and months turn quickly into years. If you use courage, hard work and have developed a network of personal relationships and are not moving up, then reconsider where you are.

Nothing wrong with realising that your genius is not recognised and that your future lies elsewhere. Your ability must be recognised with advancement. If there is no advancement then the analysis is clear.

The company feels that you are at that level of incompetence, where you will be having lunch with Mr. Stuckinarut for the rest of your career. If your advancement is passed over on two occasions, look elsewhere, unless you want to stay put or be moved towards the door.

If you believe that your non-advancement is because of a bias against your sex or race and you have the qualifications, you may address your thoughts to HR. This could cause you more problems in the future. If this is the case then move on, and ask for resolution with the courts.

Newbies

How do we do it? What kind of graduate would you hire? The smartest of her class? Middle range student? Bottom range? To hire someone out of university you are shooting the dice. Some say that the only thing that a graduate can do is learn how to pass an exam. In reality, unless the graduate has had work experience or proven his worth as a PhD then it is an unknown entity. Throwing money to the graduate with the most credentials is not good policy. You are gambling. Policy on salaries should show a gradual rise to entry-level pay over the probationary period or faster if the employee shows the capacity anticipated. If the candidate interviews as a champion then you may end up in a bidding war with competition. What are you looking for?

Degree of the talent required.
Ex university experience and accomplishment.
Letters from referees.
Work experience.
Well dressed and spoken.

Tend to be careful when prospects have squeezed through their academics. This could be the first symptom of laziness.
If the candidate is top of the scholastic year it shows hard work. Does he have the capacity to do as well as learn? If he was up all night and working at his studies 20 hours a day then he may not be the ideal. The candidate who is top of the class may have expectations to walk into a high paying position before proving himself. Let the others chase him. Unless he is obviously the best candidate and will bring revenues and savings above his position in quick time, then let it go. Candidate number two will be less expensive and will have an easier personality. Hiring just out of school requires examination not just in scholarship. Pass them through Personality Tests and basic comprehension. Someone with at least a second language is a 5 star candidate. 3 languages including Spanish and English Fantastic. Mandarin and Hindi Yes!!
If he is a middle of the road scholar, how many hours did he study a week? If the answer is between 40 and 50 hours then he will be middle of the road for salaries. He has the availability. He is used to work normal hours. He probably had other interests than school proving diverse activities. Room to develop.

There will be winners and losers during the probation periods. Using Strategic Management you will be responsible to guide them through the learning process of your company. Managing new hires with SM will lay the foundation of the best outcome possible.

Being able to laugh is one of the pleasures at work. Mature people have more experiences to laugh about. Younger ones are afraid to upset people. Using humour to get a message across can have better results than a dictate from the Boss. Create a humoristic journal of the business. It should talk about generalities within your industry, successes in finding new clients, recognising good work. If you are going to make a joke about an employee or a manager, ask for their permission first.

Put one of the office jokers in charge. Every company has one. Not a rude, or insolent exposure of people. A genuinely funny guy, respected, who shows the boss what he intends to write hits the mark. NEVER ridicule the employee. Laugh at yourself first. This should not be a journal that is edited on a weekly basis. Only send it when there is a good reason. Christmas Party, Golf Tournament, Business Enhancements. Losing the old photocopier. Retirements. New equipment. You get the picture.

Chapter 10

Your Boss.

The single most important relationship in your job is between you and your boss. It is not the customer, your workmates, your suppliers or yourself. It is not the higher up Bosses, nor the lower level Bosses. It is your Boss and she rules the nest.

She could be fantastic, super, medium, ugly, uglier, and nasty. Communicative or silent. Hard working or sloppy. Listens or ignores. Bully or soft. These are extremes, but these are the parameters where your Boss shall find herself in your eyes. What do we do to make the best of it?

Our perception of the Boss will define our actions. We want to be productive, we want to show that we can carry the responsibility given. We will meet deadlines. We will deliver what was asked, on budget, on time, without ruining your reputation by stepping on people's toes.

Never forget that the organisation decided in its infinite wisdom that she and she alone was the person qualified enough to run the show.

Now, how should you use this relationship to help move you to higher ground? How can you show the organisation that your abilities are recognised and that you need to move onward and upward?

With time your experience with Bosses will grow. You will see behaviours that are appropriate and others that are not recommended.

Bosses should behave in a manner to get the job done not to create a living hell for their subordinates. How do we manage her?

The Boss does not like;

- Surprises. Never leave them in the dark. If there is a disaster on the horizon, tell her NOW. Small problems can be discussed if you are handling a problem, but still let her know.

- Being setup. Never set-up the Boss. If you feel that if the Boss goes ahead with a project that could be demonstrably a bad idea, don't leave them to take the fall. You could get a piece of the blame. Don't be the Whipping Boy and don't pin the Whipping Boy sign on anyone else.

- Openly dissing the Boss. A dangerous pastime. If you have a beef with her then keep this opinion between both of you. If she feels that you are openly against her in public, this will not go well for you. You will be on your own as the higher-ups will neither like nor forget such behaviour. You will be walking through a minefield and openly shooting dice with your career.

- Inaccurate calculations on budgets, payrolls, weak negotiations, thievery. Be honest in all doings and keep her up to speed. Always double check calculations. Inaccuracy is not appreciated in any business.

- Reliving a file that did not go well. The lost sale. The sexual harassment case in IT department. The call-back caused by sloppy finishing work. Once over and fixed, then get on with the job. The Barrack Room Lawyers will do the reliving. Don't join that club.

- Waste the Bosses time. As we discussed, try to avoid Big Gob, the BRL, Mr. and Mrs. Social Committee wanting a half-day meeting at the weekend to discuss the Christmas Party.

- Telling tales on your fellow managers. This creates animosity between same level managers and can create a whipping boy culture for the loser.

- Failing. When the Boss fails, she's the one on the hook. It is her baby and it is her package. It could be the lack of support, lack of information, lack of preparation, organisation, direction or control. Be careful when this happens. You could be associated.

- She gets the kudos, but she gets the blame as well. She calls the shots because she takes the hits. Help the Boss.

What your Boss will like;

- Loyalty. Stand by your Boss. If you know your stuff, she will be aware of your opinion and will have briefed you on hers and this will strengthen the relationship.

- Work Performance. Punctual always, with presence, projects, projections. Being on the ball. Engage and show Fast, Firm and Fair work habits.

- Say nice things about her when warranted. The Boss needs a pat on the back. Don't be shy, this is not a public kiss up. If she has done a good job and deserves the kudos then give it. If you as a manager received the same pat from your Boss then you feel all warm and cuddly.

- When your reporters give you a Well Done Boss, it also feels pretty darn good. Sometimes it is tough to say but do it anyway. Takes seconds to say, but is a good and remembered investment.

- Give her a freebee. If you have a brilliant new idea which will reduce costs, increase revenues, bump up share price at any level you are working, especially during the early days of your career, do this; Write a synopsis of your idea. Present it your Boss and ask her opinion. It has to be doable or it won't work.

However, don't give this freebie to an incompetent Boss who doesn't understand your idea. Find a good Boss who recognises your innovation capacity.

- If your Boss stumbles for a minor mistake of her own doing, try to mitigate the misstep. Don't take the blame. Mitigate. Not too much. If it is a doozy and you are not involved. Stay quiet. Be invisible if the Boss is a dud. The Buck stops Here.

If the Boss is fired;

- If the Boss has been let go, say nothing. A decision has been taken by the higher ups. You will only give the perception that you do not agree with the decision no matter what you say. Be quiet. Be transparent. Get on with the job.

- A fired manager goes for many reasons. Not reaching goals, lack of control. Bad results. Do not get involved in gossip, hearsay, or get drawn into chats at the photocopier or the water fountain.

- You will still have work to get on with. Be professional at all times and keep performing your work as it needs to be.

- Poor performance from managers is bad for the whole organisation. They have to be led to the door. If you were one of the higher-ups, imagine what you would do. You, as a manager, would be expected to remove a blockage in the business. The higher-ups are only doing their job, the same as you. Think of them.

- You should be watching the higher-ups at all times to observe their capacity as managers. They do this as well as all managers must. to ensure the ongoing operations are on track. Higher-ups are the same as anyone else. They are expendable if non performing.

- If your Boss leaves for whatever other reason and must be replaced! It could be retirement, new company, and relocation? This could be an unknown quantity. An outside replacement? An inside department change manager? A promotion? You? Are you ready? You should be.

- Replacing someone to replace you as a manager is one of the most important activities at any managerial level. The preparation of a replacement is a must. The manager who does not plan and organise the relief is not doing his job. Don't be shy to ask your Boss if you can replace her in meetings that she has little interest in. Show an interest in any file that looks problematic or difficult. Ask to be a part of the solution.

- Show the high and mighty that you have the interest and maybe the capacity to show your commitment. If you don't you will be forgotten. Be ready to see opportunities and get involved.

Boss Behaviour. When you are the Boss you can communicate in certain ways. How do you give a rebuke? How does the Boss react in bad times or good times? Are they stable in their style of management? Does she have favourites?

- Is your Boss is hated by everybody, or are they loved like your mother? This is the litmus test for all managers. If they are despised they will have difficulty in their work. Their decisions may be ridiculed and difficult to implement, and the perception of their personality will be one of bad manners, rudeness and bad temperedness. These perceptions will stick. To resolve and change will take years of work, and may go on forever.

- If the employees love them it may show a lack of supervision. Rules are loose. Timekeeping isn't respected, deliverables are late. We need a balance.

- If the manager is known as 'The Boss ', it is a sign that the employees are genuinely fond of her. Good managers ensure that their profile remains loyal with the three F's. Be Firm, Fair and Fast in all your doings. Using the 3 F's make you consistent, transparent and on an even keel. The best managers I have ever worked with were sold on this and used it every day.

- The litmus test for a good boss is very easy and can give you a good idea to their management style very quickly. If the manager is constantly giving out repercussions to their reporters. A constant barrage of, 'no not this!', or, 'do it again, properly!', or, 'this is the last time!', it shows a lack of empathy and understanding of basic management principles.

- If a Manager cannot speak in normal, clear and precise language then how can the reporters understand their performance requirements. How do employees react to this? They don't. Constant rebukes quickly go in one ear and out the other. Eventually rebukes become useless. They become so common they have no effect. If the manager uses rebukes only when necessary then the weight is much more effective.

- The manager who uses rebuke sparingly will generally be helpful, understanding, honest and adult. When she uses a rebuke, the employee will take the rebuke seriously. Classic good management.

- A good Boss will never reprimand an employee in front of anyone. To reprimand with an audience will install fear in all the employees. Those who witness and those who will hear about it later at the water fountain. The perception towards your loyalty, Boss, Job, Company will be lost forever. There is no faster way to completely demotivate anyone who has been dressed down in front of his co-workers by a manager.

- The Boss has to manage every employee differently. Strategic management, once understood, is used to ensure that the development of everyone can be managed according to the experience and learning curve of each reporter based on motivation and knowledge. When we observe a good manager they will use different behaviours to different employees. Pushing them, educating them, listening to them, give a mandate and leave them to it. Their level of motivation and knowledge will determine the speed and accuracy of productivity levels.

- Big Head Bosses are ten a penny. They are the Rude Boys of management. They are rude because they can be. Mr. Big Shot who has been around and has reached the pinnacle of his department can be rude because he is the top man. He usually acts like this when the culture he worked his way up the ladder with, was de rigour. It's all he knew. Now we have to live with it. You can be rude without caring whom you diss. You are at the top of the pile and you feel invincible. HR departments are fighting this.

- When the rude Boss is the founder or the owner, generally in a smaller organisation, then watch-out. Yelling, shouting, swearing, forcing overtime, sexual overtones are common. Get Out. If you are in a situation where this kind of behaviour exists then go to a lawyer. There is no need for this anywhere. Governments of today have legislated protections against abuse in the workplace. You have rights.

- Bosses who have favourites. Not a good scenario. This implies that there are whipping boys and the preferred crowd. This creates a dysfunctional environment where there is misery for some who are unheard and others who are calling the shots. To rectify the situation let's take the manager out to another department and replace him with a manager who has no favourites. This will reset the manager culture immediately. It gives a shot across the bow to the outgoing manager and shows the incoming manager a pat on the back once the problem is fixed.

- I have worked with companies who have certain managers who have expertise and are used for certain scenarios. Tough Guy for Achieving Deadlines. Smooth Guy when delicate negotiations are required. Numbers Guy when sales are not reaching goals. Swapping the right trait manager around to where they are required saves money and time.

- Boss Credentials. Bosses are very pleased when they have quotable credentials. *I worked at IBM for twenty years. Yes, I have an MBA from the LSE.* Wow, I'm impressed. People will not care where you worked or which piece of paper you received from a guy with a funny hat if you don't perform. No matter your pedigree, a Manager is only as good as his present performance.

- Do we really care about the number of books in her office or the number of certificates there are on the office wall? I mean, really? You can buy these on the Internet. I have a Degree in Mickey Mouse Studies from The University of Laughs. It cost twenty bucks. That would impress me, but then again, I have not looked at any of the papers, dissertations, reports or textbooks read at school that I have kept stuck in the corner of a wardrobe in my bed room since I graduated. Didn't look at anything. Formulas? No. Economics? No. The most valuable insights and methodology exposed to me were on the job. So why bother?

- My Father used to tell me that a University Degree only shows that the student could pass exams. Practicing what you have learned and applying what you studied is another deal altogether. Every project, file, negotiation, training, book, paper has been far more difficult to finalise and install than anything that I did at school. I should empty my wardrobe of all my papers and books, because I never had a gander at them. I'm too busy to read them and they are out-dated. I get on with the job.

Bad Boss

- Is slow to ask for help from superiors
- Resents authority
- Has favourites in the workforce
- Is late
- Suspicious of innovations
- Keeps secrets
- Avoids meetings
- Can't see the future

Good Boss

- Has daily contacts with higher ups to solicit support
- Welcomes aid offered with eyes and ears open
- Treats all subordinates exactly the same
- Is on time, prepared and open to work
- Lobbies for innovation in technology and methodology
- Entrenches good ideas from interior or exterior sources
- Regularly informs the staff of work status
- Uses official and unofficial channels of communication daily
- Has a budget and business model for the year

Chapter 11

Nepotism?

Tough question. It exists in almost every organisation in the world. Family businesses of course, but we will find them in Governments, Non-Profits, Large Companies. Partnerships. Try and find an organisation that doesn't. Wives, sons, daughters, brothers, sisters, best friends, and old friends, school chums. Charlie from the golf club. Anita, the wife of Bobby from the Lodge. Mona, married to the Boss.

How do we behave with the favoured?

Well, there is not much we can do. On many occasions you may be working hand in hand with a favoured one. How do you know who is favoured or not. If the relationship has never been revealed then naming a nepotism relationship may be told to one themself. If you spout out that you feel that a favoured was chosen for a post, you could be letting another aware of your feelings. It's best to say nothing. Do your job. Praise those that deserve it. Remand those who deserve it. Even if you are giving the CEO's daughter a remanding you have to do it. That is your job and that is why you hold that position. Treat all employees and higher ups as the same whether or not they are the Bosses aunt or the stepson of the Head Accountant. You may want to get your son a job there one day. Ask most people in the organisation, would they want that I treat their son the same as everyone else? Of course.

I was managing a Real Estate office and my 16-year-old son needed a summer job. So, I hired him as a data entry clerk in the back office. An easy job. It wasn't a lucrative position and it could be boring. I soon realised that it would be a short tenure. His supervisor, our Administrative Manager called me on the first day. 'Sorry to tell you that Taylor showed up an hour late this morning.' I thanked her and called Taylor. 'What time did you arrive at the office?' '10am. Sorry. It won't happen again.' OK. Two days later I got the same call. Taylor's career at the office was done. The news went around that the Boss had just fired his son.

The Manager had done her job. I thanked her and I gave Taylor a lecture in workplace behaviour. That is the way to treat nepotism in an organisation. You, as a manager must treat ALL employees in exactly the same fashion. If you treat the favoured, don't think that the workforce won't know. They will. Sure, I can try and hide it at the beginning, but eventually they will find out.

By letting bad management or poor performance be looked over and by letting things go you will suffer a background of resentment from other employees. This can cause a devastating atmosphere that could change the good culture that has been installed. Changing the culture of an organisation is one of the most difficult and dangerous projects to undertake. I have seen death spirals start in an organisation because of nepotism that had not been stopped when the penny dropped. A manager must remove nepotism immediately it starts to hurt the business,

Better if you don't drop in people who are not qualified, or who you know. It is prudent to have a policy which disallows nepotism altogether.

Then there is the company, which openly hires and promotes family and friends even if they are not qualified for the position. My advice is then to find another job.

If you want to move ahead and eventually be a higher-up, then don't wait for a miracle. No matter how proficient, professional and loyal you are, Uncle Charlie will get the job. Find something fast and run to the door, don't walk.

Nepotism will be present as long as organisations are. From Royal Families to Mom and Pop Convenience stores. Learn to live with them. If you are happy. Be Fair, be Firm, be True. However if you want to advance, get out.

Chapter 12

Things you can be fired for.

When the meeting is of a disciplinary quality with a subordinate then there are elements that we should apply and others, which must be avoided. Meetings to give out discipline should be of a consistent manner. I have worked with managers whose planning in disciplinary matters consisted of intimidation with threats to the subordinates losing their job, pension plan, suspension and instilling fear to a point that they are incapable of achieving their mandates.

Various threats and prehistoric techniques to change behaviour do not work. Phrases to avoid are;

- We are now talking. Next we will write. If this continues, then we will hit!
- This is not a dialogue. This is a monologue!
- One last chance.
- Do you like your job?
- We've had enough of your shenanigans!

Threats will not resolve any unwanted behaviour. Simple traits from employees, which need to be resolved in the simplest cases such as;

- Tardiness (the biggest)
- Breaking Policies
- Improperly using assets
- Falsely stating time sheets
- Falsely reporting expense accounts

These are minor offences. Major ones are of a different animal, the solution to minor discrepancies in behaviour is a relatively simple and quickly resolved.

Once the infringement has been reported to yourself you must ensure that the episode is valid and observed. It must be recorded in the file of the employee. You, as the immediate supervisor, must inform HR of the infraction and of the steps that you intend to apply in the case. Always make sure that HR is aware of the situation. They will be able to guide you and ensure that any employment laws active in your jurisdiction are respected. Also, inform your immediate supervisor, with an email, before meeting the employee.

If you work in a company that has Union representation then there will be a written agreement between the company and the Union as to employee warnings from initial problems to termination. In Union environments employee discipline is far more complexes than a non-Union one.

When there is no Union agreement it is the Labour laws of the jurisdiction, which applies, and it is here that the HR department of the organisation earns its money.

There MUST be an annexe in the employment contract which states what happens in the case of insubordination and to which levels. An example could be that if it is a case of administrative leave than the employee could be paid, while a theft suspicion will be considered without pay. Each suspension, depending on the fault of the employee will be required to spell out the conditions of the suspension.

On occasion we learn that employees have been extremely bad. Suspension without pay could be designated while HR and management find the circumstances, the degree of insubordination and consider the penalty to be applied.

A behaviour that could apply a suspension without pay could be;

- Theft
- Selling assets of the company
- Sexual Harassment
- Threatening violence
- Drug consumption on the job

These are of course very serious. This behaviour is rare but not impossible to experience.

In the day-to-day management of your reporters, you will have to deal with the more mundane types of control as we have mention before. This requires a swift, easy, strategy, which should fix the situation.

No matter whom you are dealing with the punishment for any low level offence, which requires a rebuke, is quick and emotional for the employee. No one likes to get a mouthful from the Boss. When it is a talk with a disappointed Boss who believes in the employee, then it sinks in and is remembered.

As mentioned before when the manager meets someone in her office, there is a protocol for meeting. This meeting to give discipline is the same. Shake hands. Give a cordial greeting. Get to Business.

'Do you know why I asked to see you today?'

'Is it about my lateness-lack of productivity-too much playing on the internet-yakking at the coffee machine-calling in sick the 20th time-bungling the easy sale-bad mouthing the company?'

'Yes. That is why. Please explain to me what happened.'

'Well, My kid missed his school bus-I've been overwhelmed with the new software-I like to chat with workmates-I'm going through my menopause-they didn't want to buy-other companies have better benefits!'

Some answers may be valid. So you have to be sure that when giving a warning whether verbal or written, that it is valid in all cases.

If the warning is valid ask the following question.

'I have confidence in you to respect the rules and regulations of the business. They are in place for a reason. **How do you think it makes me feel when I hear about your behaviour?'**

Stay silent for 30 seconds.

The employee will not reply.

Say, 'I'm counting on you. I know we won't have to speak about this again. Thank you.'

Get up. She will get up. When she is up, take her by the elbow toward the door. Just before the door, still by the elbow, say again, 'I'm counting on you.'

This simple statement will pull at the emotion of the employee. They know the answer.

Place a report of the meeting in the file of the employee and inform HR of the meeting you had.

When there is a Union environment in the organisation then all employees who are members must be managed according to the agreement between the parties. Unions have lost a lot of ground during the last forty years. Membership has fallen in all major industries where they were historically strong, due to automation, technology and better working conditions without union intervention.

Dishing out punishments to employees depend on many facets. They could be administrative based on lack of work, re-organisation of the organisation, loss of revenues, loss of a contract, new owners or bankruptcy.

These events normally have no input from you. These are consequences, which are out of your control.
Your behaviour on the job and on certain occasions will get you fired.

Allegations of Sexual Harassment. In today's environment, this is the deadliest pill you can take. At no time is this behaviour appropriate. Do not do this under any circumstance. Men will be denounced, with no judgement. They disappear.

Stealing company assets. You cannot do this. This is theft. Not is it only against company policy, stealing is a felony.

Passing along confidential company information to third parties. Not even to your spouse, friend, and relative. No.

Threatening an employee or a customer. Bad. Police. Criminal.

You, as a manager, cannot blurt out 'Your Fired!' like the shows on TV. There is a process, which needs to be followed to ensure a legal, recorded process, which is transparent and well documented. HR will be required to be involved. You must inform your immediate supervisor. If the process deals with an Unionised employee then the Union must be informed. Previous events associated with the employee must be considered during the study. Any discrepancy in the employee's previous behaviour must be recorded and held in their HR file. The behaviour of the HR managers of the file must follow the employment laws to the letter to ensure its application and ensure that the rights of the employee are followed.

Depending on the jurisdiction where your organisation is located, you will have your own set of laws and regulations that apply to you. Learn them.

During a termination process I was involved in, we had enough information to end the employment of an entry-level employee. She was tardy, ineffective, and rude to employees and customers. She had received several verbal and written warnings about her behaviour and lack of production with no improvement. HR was informed. Her manager informed me and I informed my manager, who authorised the termination. Her manager and a member of HR met the employee, gave her the letter of termination and took her to the door. She complained and reported that she would seek retribution from lawyers and government agencies. Guess what? She got her job back by an admin mistake. Everything we had done to manage the process was by the book, except for one detail. The letter of termination was dated the day before it was presented to her. That date was her day off. The Tribunal responsible for Employment Law decided that because the letter had been dated on her day off then the action was not valid. You can't fire someone on his or her day off. We had to reinstate her with back pay and forfeit a tidy sum. Be attentive that everything in the file is solid, true, well documented.
Go over everything with a steel comb. Analyse everything before action. HR took the hit because they dictated the letter. Be assured that any letter not written by myself in the future, that I was a part of, receives my full attention.

When a firing happens, it is not usually for a slight episode. Some cases involve behaviour that can't be shared with the employees. This can be difficult for managers.
Confidentiality can hurt or aid the organisation. If the target was an unliked manager, then the employees tend to be happy about her ouster. If a well liked manager who was on the take for years, then ousted, the secret will not stay quiet for long.

An episode where good guys are stealing comes as a shock to the workforce. I have been present several times where the good guy has been on the take. As a generalisation, the least probable culprit is your man. Beware who arrives too early and leaves too late. The cashier who has open pockets. One of the greatest disappointments to any organisation is when a respected, competent, liked by all, senior manager is given the boot for pilfering.

If you discover that there are assets missing either from intuition or from actions that looked suspicious then there is something wrong and you must investigate and react. Not all companies have sergeants at arms or large security divisions so you as a manager may be left holding the file.

People who tend to be on the take are…..everyone working for you.

Some will swipe office supplies. Ink for a printer. Paper. Pens. Computer parts.

Some will swipe copies of software, screens, and product.

Some will swipe cash.

If the assets are cash, computers, TV screens, or anything else of value, the hit is on the balance sheet of the company and hurting the assets.

Human nature will bend the will of people where there is opportunity that is easily available. First order of business is outlining company policy in the signed conditions of employment stating the punishment for thievery. There is only one. The sack. You must investigate and be sure of your facts. You must have 100% facts. Tell your Boss. Suspend the employee without pay. Reaffirm with other employees in the affected department. Try to have a smoking gun. Do you call the police? If the monies belong to the company then that depends. If the monies are of a large amount then maybe. Will the PR problem of the theft be disclosed?

A company may decide to let the employee go, but don't act to avoid bad PR. These parameters will have to be disclosed to the managers. What level of tolerance, if any, should be tolerated. If the monies belong to the public domain, the theft should be reported to the police.

Danger people can be anyone, including;

Employees who work alone with little supervision.

An accountancy employee who never takes a day off. He arrives first and leaves last. Has his paperwork in place and in advance. Check his work by a random timetable. Check his work the day after you checked it last. Surprise audits.
Security checks at manufacturing centers. Employees who arrive with empty bags and leave with full ones.
Employees leaving on vacation the fifth time this year.
Nice cars.
Dressing well.
Rolex.
Diamond Anything.

Obviously not all signs of living well will indicate some naughty business of the employee. He may be married to a lawyer or doctor. But if it is budget secretary then you may have a problem.

Personally, I believe that unions are good and bad depending on the leadership of the Union. An intelligent, serious leader who is a well-respected senior worker who can deal with management, understanding that there is already in place a good convention may deal to change at the next agreement sessions.

With newly placed negotiators the inexperienced negotiator will demand over the top conditions. In my experience I have negotiated with Unions on bargaining agreements. The negotiations were always a great mystery to me that they would be drawn out the longest time for the slightest of improvements. Huge changes would be demanded on schedules with fewer hours worked for more money. Even when calculations were shown to the union representatives that it couldn't work they would run off in the huff for a long weekend. Meanwhile their members were sitting at home with no work. Every negotiation during a strike generally will give a positive cash flow to the members if the strike or lockout was a duration of 7 days or less. I have never seen an

agreement where this was done. Once I experienced a strike of one full summer. The members had no salary for 3 months meanwhile the negotiating team had their salary paid by the Union, and took vacation during the process.
It takes a special employee to take on Union negotiations. Some take days, others months.

Every word, every full stop, every comma in the final agreement between the organisation and the Union represents dollars and cents. The Unions' perception of management is trying to squeeze longer hours for less money, while the Managements perception is the opposite. Whether it is extra vacation days, less sick days, safer working conditions, longer lunch breaks, bigger lockers, the two parties will be at polar positions at the onset.

Who do we put in charge for negotiations? As a manager you will require;

- A Lawyer in Labour Law
- A Representative of HR
- A Manager involved in the Operations and Finance
- The Manager who works on a daily basis with Industrial Relations

This negotiating committee will report directly to the higher-ups who will call the final shots. They will crunch the numbers that are needed to say yes, its possible to no, it's hopeless.

If an issue is brought up by the Union and the negotiating team start to respond to it then that issue will become a part of the final agreement. Either in this round of talks or as an add-on or during the next negotiation. If new subjects are permitted to be entered then you will at some point be stuck with it.

Know what you DONT want. Every time the Union tries to insert a dialogue about the subject, you must blank it. We don't open that file. Point. If the subject is accepted then each negotiation will try to expand the initial agreement. Holiday Pay, Overtime, Sick Days. This negotiation will be for 10 days of Sick Time. Next will be 15 days. Next will be 20 days. Where will it end? Once the snowball starts down the hill, when it hits the bottom, the ball that could be held in the hand will be the size of an SUV.

If Government Officials are asked to intervene in negotiations by a Union, then the principal negotiators may find that the resulting agreements may be pro or con the Unions depending on the presiding Political Parties. When an interjection by a political personage is given, then you are assured that she will side on the best outcome possible to boost her popularity with the electorate.

Political interference is problematic. If this happens to you, back off. You wont have the weight required to make a stand. Send the problem upstairs.

If you have a strike at your workplace and you are the one calling the shots be aware of certain characteristics;

- Normally a strike means that the strikers will not be paid. If the strike lasts two weeks or more then the strikers will never recuperate the earnings lost.
- You take the chance that media will take an interest in your strike and it becomes public. The Union certainly wants attention to their plight, and you can too. You must be able to defend your position with sound argument, numbers and the plight of your customers. If you have to do this for TV cameras, radio microphones, and web-portals then stand tall and be articulate.

The Manager who works daily with the Union is an important hire. She will be someone who can laugh with the Union members, who is respected by the Union inner circle. This could be an ex Union member who evolved within the Organisation and knows the inner workings of such an entity, and has proven herself as a solid member of management. These managers are few and far between. When you have one, guard her well. She will be a godsend when negotiations become slow and blocked. She will shorten the distance between the two parties and understand their concerns. An ability to communicate their officious demands to management in a clear and concise manner.

The greatest malaise in Union/Management communications is the protection of bad employees by the union. 90% of union time is taken up by the protection of 5% of the employees. The unions know these people well. They report to them every day to complain about anything they can think of. I grew up in a socialist country. Unions were strong because they had to be. Workplaces were dangerous. Long hours were not paid by overtime. Layoffs and mass firings were commonplace. Maternity leave was non-existent. Unions were needed.

The evolution of Unions is one of decreasing membership. Workers rights have improved over the years to the point of excellent quality of conditions and advancements. Protection of ne'er do wells does not show any Union has progressed.

Language and Understanding

As a young man I travelled extensively. My first real jump was from Glasgow to London. I had saved some money from a summer job. I was 18 years old, I was determined to go there and take my share of the gold pavements.
Unfortunately when I got there the golden pavements were nowhere to be seen. On arriving I found myself with: no food; no drink; no bed; no job; no nothing.

Have you ever heard a Scottish person who could communicate with the English, with no understanding between the two? I could generally understand what they were saying, but I was unintelligible at best. My words, sentences and exclamations were unheard. My English friends called my accent 'Talking bollocks.' And they were right.

I learned my lesson very quickly.

Simply put, if my message is not crystal clear to those that need the information, then I am at fault.

I spoke in a very broad Scottish accent, and assumed that every English speaker could easily understand me. However, even if a Scottish accent was reasonably understood by most English speakers, my accent was impossible to translate. I had a Glasgow accent and as such had no chance of making myself understood.

I found work through an Irishman who promised me a job at a building site. I was 18, strong, and obviously keen.

The foreman promised a week long try-out and a yes or no decision at the end of the week. At the end he called me to the cabin and gave me some bad news. He said,' Robin, we like you, but for God's sake we can't understand a word you say. Sorry but you have to go.' Naturally I was very upset. The money was good, and I was working outside in London, which was a thrill every day.

The foreman saw my disappointment, as I pled for a prolongation.

He then gave me one of the most important teachings of my life.

The foreman said, ' I see your disappointment. I'll give you one more week here, but we have a communication problem. We have a worker here called Alf. If you want to talk to me for anything, then you have to speak to him first. Do you agree?'

Of course I said OK to keep my job. 'Anything to keep working!'

I spoke to Alf. I asked him if he wanted a cup of tea. When he spoke I couldn't understand a word he said. I laughed and took my lesson home.

I came to work the next day speaking English with expert pronunciation, grammar and clear vocabulary. I learned my lesson.

It is not OK for us to insist that our communication is the only one that applies. We must in all occasions ensure that we make ourselves understood and communicate to all of our colleagues in the most understandable language possible.

If they don't understand, it is our fault. Not theirs.

Chapter 13

Sleeping with the Payroll.

DO NOT sleep with the payroll. This will cause you no end of trouble. The gossips will have a ball. Nepotism rumours will abound. Your Boss will not be happy. You will lose on so many fronts.
First of all I would expect that any hanky-panky between employees are semi ok. Chemistry and attraction and hormones work all the time. Normally they will ask for the same shifts and the same vacations. There is, in the beginning usually no conflict at this level. But, it's still not good.

Managers sleeping with their subordinates are another kettle of fish. Scenarios, real or imagined by the employees in the department will always be considered real. Favourites will be made and accused. Animosity will be bolstered as rumours of favouritism are thrown around. Protection of the junior will cause problems with other managers. Rumours will whizz around the organisation. This is a spectacle that the business doesn't need. These things never end well. What happens at the end of the relationship? Who needs to be transferred? These sideshows have no place in our productivity.

Beware of favouritism, nepotism, overlooking errors and protectionism. If there are couples that appear in the same department, move one of them. If the relationship goes well then it's lovey dovey over the printer. If this goes bad then there is emotional baggage that has to be resolved.

Move one of them out. Fast. You will be happy that you did.

Chapter 14

Operational Procedures and Budgets

All departments in any business should have a document based on the work of the department called Operational Procedures. This is the guidebook of what you do.

It explains all the situations that may arise in the day-to-day business of the department. Who is responsible for which procedure. Who is authorised to do what?

What reports are required and delivered to whom. Basically whatever happens in the department.

If you inherit one, on arrival of your new position, you can show that the company was right in hiring you by;

Demanding a revision of the operational procedures, compiled by junior managers with input from front-line employees.

With your most competent manager, explore the produced document and have her validate the information.

Send the document to your Boss with your and the managers name on the document.

Collect the Operational Procedures of all departments in the business that overlaps with your department. If they are more than one year old, or there has been exceptional growth ask if you can revise the documentation with the overlapping department. You will be seen as a go-getter.

You will have in short thrift updated the operational procedures, motivated your best manager to new heights and validated your managers' trust.

Budgets

Every year you will normally have to deposit a budget with the finance department. Many managers are afraid of budgets. Creating a huge spreadsheet with cost centers and a full declaration of every red cent accounted for is, I believe, over the top.

Budgets are relatively easy. There shouldn't be giving you the sweats or palpitations.

Ask the finance department what we should be aiming for. They will tell you....Max 5% across.....With the new Union agreement 7.5%......
This makes budgets easy. Take last years real budget and add 5% or tie it to the Government Bank Rate.

However this methodology can be pretty simple and even though it is going to be around this quick guesswork needs tweaking.

You have to check the last three years budget to ensure itemised cost centers are on line. For example there will always be outstanding elements. For example there could have been;

A fire at the plant.
A summer long strike
A large fine from the Government
Supply Chain failures
Unexpected stock buy back
New product out performs market

Department Heads will have input from finance. They will know and you should be aware from the unofficial gossip that the Board of Directors will always cut the Budget proposed by 7.5%.

When depositing your budgets for the year to the Finance Officer you will need the following documents. Every organisation will have budget software that will make it a lot easier. If you don't know the software then learn it. To have an understandable conversation with your colleagues, you will need it.

Employee costs. (New employees, lost employees, changes to Union contracts)
IT upgrade costs (Software, Upgrades to Hardware)
Leasing
Raw materials
Consultants
Customer recruitment
Discounting
Advertising
Client arrears

Employee costs as in salaries have to be competitive in your industry. Pay less than anyone else then you will not attract the best. Pay too much and you are not good at what you do. Be fair. Be realistic. Make sure that your employees are paid correctly. Don't be lazy about this. Make the right call. On bonus, Holiday pay, and performance. If you have employees with the same salary level, time on the job, and job title each one should have their own compensation. Evaluation procedures have to be in place, but as we are dealing with people of different attributes, compensation will be supple across the board. If you pay an under achiever the same as a productive member of the team, then the poorer quality member will feel happy that they got away with it. Don't let this happen. Money can be a tool to underscore a missing part of their competence. Tell them about this as soon as you detect it. Don't surprise them at their evaluation interview.
Managers who don't treat compensation matters in this way are lazy and create distrust and lack of motivation among his subordinates.

In every budget there will be changes all throughout the financial year. If we had a crystal ball to see every event then we wouldn't need to run a business, we could stay at home and make bets on events. But, this is not our lot. We have to manage. Take your pick as to what can happen. The answer is nothing and everything and everything in between the two. The Cunard Line didn't expect that the Titanic would sink on neither its yearly budget, nor the automobile industry in 2008.

Chapter 15

Managing by walking around.

The finest managers I have known and worked with had similar traits. Organised. Available. Constant communication. Never, ever reprimand someone in public. Visible and on time.

One of the traits that I quickly adopted was managing by walking around.

Every day, without fault, whether a five minute quickie or a one hour promenade throughout the plant, office, dining room, kitchen, sales floor. Talk to your people. Say Hello to every employee you meet.

Know their names (Yes. Really. Know their names.) Ask them questions about their jobs. Any bad news, any good news. People always feel good after they had a good word with the boss.

It must be bad news, before good news. Always. Your staff will not feel this, but they remember the good news more than the bad when you use this method and they leave with a better taste.

Ask about their family, Kids at school, The Job.
Look and see who is working. Is there anyone not working? Find a place where you can't be seen easily. Have a looksee where you are not easily detected. You will see what goes on.

Employee's behaviour is usually not what is on stage when you are present. So be clandestine, but not all the time. If you see waste going on speak to the manager of that department. Do not go directly to the employee. It is the manager's job to reprimand. If you see exceptionally good behaviour, tell the manager. Make sure that the Manager tells the employee about his good behaviour.

Don't get involved with past beefs or subjects that have already been decided by arbitration or by Union negotiations. Subjects that have been resolved by competent agencies are out of bounds.

If the employee has an idea that concerns work ask him to submit to you an outline of the idea on paper. Just the idea. Not schematics, budgets or a project spreadsheet. Just one sheet with the general outline. Give the paper to the person who should see it. It could be something really simple that saves time and money.

If it costs nothing but improves the business then great. Pat on the back and if possible, make it happen. Front line employees have ideas. Good and bad. If it looks do-able and the manager in charge of the activity says so, try it for a short period and get the feedback of the users.

Walking around is effective on every level. Official communications from the Higher-Ups is needed for clarity and guidance. Unofficial communications are more important when delivered by someone in person. On the level. Person to person. You will receive more respect and be listened if you mirror the employee in your eye-to-eye contact.

Do it.

Chapter 16

Doing things

To be a manager is to do what?

It's a pretty simple idea. Realise your mandate to make things better and innovate to make our work easier, faster and more productive.

Reduce Costs and Increase Sales.

Some managers have difficulty with this. Innovation is a tough cookie to crack and many managers will fall at the hurdle of innovation.
It's not that they are not good managers.
We tend to specialise over time.
We are better at people management, but hopeless at finance.
We have the project plan down to the hour and dollar, but have difficulty with the staff. To be an all rounder when you are the boss is to try and specialise as quickly as possible.
Learn from the guys who are the experts.
When I work with managers who are obviously better than me in certain disciplines I ask to sit in with them when they do their magic.
Flattery will invite you to her office. Tell her the goods you need from her.

Listen and learn.

Ask her what she needs from you, and then give it.

My expertise was always HR, sales and innovation. I would talk to my fellow managers, subordinates, and colleagues and share what I knew. Then I listened to them. I learned about IT, Union management and negotiation, HR management, start up management and Finance all from listening and watching the appropriate expert that I worked with.

In return I would give them the good common sense that I have learned with over 44 years of management experience. Sharing experience is the sweetest fruit of knowledge. What works, and what doesn't. Share it.

Have a scrum every month with your fellow managers. One hour to swap an experience and share the resolution you applied or the disaster that unfolded by your inability to resolve a situation.

It's a bit like the AA.

'Hi, My name is Robin. Last week I was missing two guys on the quality control of the flight simulator XE332. I didn't check the staff needed, and two customers came by to see it and we didn't have the people there to show them.' Ouch.
Or 'I gave an engineer a written warning last week without informing HR or the Union.' Ouch. Or, ' We have initiated an employees suggestion to cut costs by 3% by eliminating a part of the process which was defunct.' Sweet.

A manager's life is one of mystery. At any time the Higher-Ups may decide that you have the capacity to manage another department, whether on the same level to where you are or to move on up.
If you are downgraded a department, start to look for something else.

I arrived at a new business where I was a shoe in for three departments. All were operational, but for three separate departments completely. I had the most experience and knowledge in Canada and was available. I was hired without portfolio. Then after a month I was asked which operation I would like to head up. Another question was also posed. Which operation did I not want to head up?
I knew which one I did not want to head up.
The Higher Ups gave me the job I said I didn't want.
So I did it for four years. I hated it.

Be prepared when you join an organisation. You never know where you will end up. If you are a manager, you may be a specialist. But in many circumstances you will be a manager where you are expected to be polyvalent. The department doesn't matter. You could be assigned to finances, marketing, operations, and administration. You are expected to do the job. If you are short on knowledge or have little experience on your mandate do what thousands have done before you.
Fake it till you make it.

Learn fast. Find resources. Find a mentor. Get up to speed.
If you are smart and not lazy you will succeed. Don't be afraid. Look ahead and trust your technical people. Trust all your people until they trip up.

If you have a subordinate who has difficulties make a mental note.
Observe and check his output and scan for errors.
If nothing bad happens over a month, let it go.
If there is a repetition then take him off the job and do it your self.
He will notice. If he stands up to you and asks why you completed the task yourself, let him be aware that he will have to buck up his performance.
Ask him of he needs any help. This is an important question.
The answer will define him.

The answer is of course, yes. A no reply puts him on the clock.
If he wants help, give it. He will try to achieve the right result.
Do not tolerate repeated mistakes. After all, the Higher Ups will not like bad calculations, increased absenteeism or poor expense management coming out of YOUR department.

Catch it and Fix it. Make it whole again. If the subordinate just can't do it then move him towards the door.

If you have developed your people, those who report to you should ask you frequently,

- 'Why don't we change this?'
- 'We can do better than this process.'
- 'We can save money by doing XYZ.'
- 'XY Inc. is beating us because they have implemented better software.'

There will be occasions when someone on your staff will come up with an idea. As soon as you hear a suggestion that will increase sales or reduce cost without harming the product, tell them, 'OK. Show me.' '

Give them the job. Let her run with it. Is she a go-getter? You might have a genius. You might have a grump who complains a lot. When your people ask for an improvement, they will have to prove to you their capacities. The grumps and Barrack Room Lawyers will not ask any questions. All you will hear from them is complaints, 'That will never work' or 'Your dreaming!'

Your best people will come up with innovation because it is in their profile. Your best will want change, move everything forward.

The no interest doozies and the Barrack Room Lawyers will complain about any change big or small.

You will have some homework to do. Tell them to outline the idea. Cost out the process. Show deadlines for key deliverables; Give them the tools that they will need. Encourage them. If it all looks good, show it to your boss and give the author the credit. They came up with it. You will get some kudos, but the spotlight should be on the creator. This is a part of your job. Encourage the creators of innovation.

This is the unofficial way that innovation is brought into the organisation. Innovation can also be brought in through R and D departments or by the order of the Board.

By encouraging our own people in direct line with our business to innovate makes us proud of our achievements. It feels good.

Spread the genius of your employees.

Chapter 16

Software

Things have changed since 1984. Ah, the good old days. The latest technological apparatus we had was a fax machine, and a big ass photocopier. The admin would go nuts if they found someone sending a fax without their permission. Then DOS came along. Then IBM cuddled up to Microsoft and we had computers running on DOS.

I was working in the Caribbean at the time. Our outfit was Hotel and Casino operations. There was no University or Technical College on the island. However I was desperate to get on the Computer Bandwagon that was just getting off the ground. So I went to Miami and bought myself a Commodore 64. This was fantastic. I had a spreadsheet, not unlike a prehistoric Excel. The spreadsheet was enclosed by plastic box the size of a brick and had to be plugged into the Commodore. I had a word processor that was like writing in gobbledegook, there were so many keys to make capitals and dashes and numbers…arrgh…Took some time but I was getting it. Then one day I was reading the local newspaper. The town High School had placed an ad for a DOS beginner's class. What luck! I was the first in line, as I expected that there would be a huge demand for this. Finally there were only 4 of us who signed up. The professor was an Irish lad, and the course was confusing, difficult and frustrating. I could understand the Prof because my Scottish accent was similar to his, while the Island Boys really didn't get it and they soon left.

I was soon on the team that was elaborating computer friendly infrastructures and support on innovative solutions. It's good to be in the right place at the right time. I became the IT guy and never looked back. I had no idea what I was doing. I was ahead by a head of the knowledge required, or as we say, I was the one eyed man in the land of the blind.

Sometimes that's all it takes.

When a company starts up and consider a decision for software that has to be made. In House software or contract the software to a supplier.
As a manager you have several options. There are good and bad reasons on both sides of the decision making process.
All the CEO's who I know personally have the same beef.
Once you start the process of an in-house solution you are tied forever.
It will grow like an always-hungry monster, an insatiable elephant in the Boardroom. Gobbling up more and more of the company's assets.
The ever-crying baby that keeps you awake at night.
Many regret the decision, wishing that the required solution had been contracted out, or the software just bought.
The dream is that the in house solution will be sold on and become a profit center in itself.
The opposite side of course is that we are supplying the competition.
Think carefully on this decision. Make projections of an increase of 33% costs on a straight line per year.
Will your revenues increase by sharing the software?
Is there a similar product existing?
Make the cost calculation of staff, recourses, space, and time.
If it doesn't work compared to your efforts you will find that you will be ahead with contracting out the software, with no pains for you.
It becomes the supplier's headache.
Be aware of this when signing a lease. Ensure your upper hand on delivery dates and ongoing updates and fixes

Chapter 17

Litigation

Be smart about litigation problems. Some industries go through life with little or no problems with the law. Taxes are paid. Conflicts are settled between adults. Honest mistakes are settled by mutual respect between Organisations.
In many countries around the world avoidance of litigation is the norm. Reasonableness is de rigour and is part of the culture.
Litigation in North America is a daily minefield of threats and semi-ridiculous claims of unfair practices. The only winners in any litigation are those in the law industry. The most common practice is that the entity with the deepest pockets in their litigation budget (yes, they exist), or has an insurance policy that covers legal fees, will win in the long run. Time will dictate the process that you can suffer. Time will kill you slowly. If your process will take longer than a year to resolve, settle reasonably on either side of the law.

It's not a case of admitting wrongdoing. It's not pleading guilt. It's saving the company in many circumstances. If you have a lawyer on contingency then you will be able to prolong the case. If the case is stuck or wont move along then swallow the problem. If the litigation asked for is between 1% and 2% of your yearly profit, do it, and move on. Any company in Europe should be receiving litigation on average once every 10 years. In North America, expect every 3 years. What's the lesson here? Make sure that you have litigation insurance if you have operations in North America.

The vast majority of litigation in North America is settled out of court. Due to the huge sums demanded by the plaintiff, companies hire the lawyers to settle early and reasonably. The sums offered might be a few thousand dollars compared to the hundreds of thousands, which may be offered by a judge who is up for re-election that year. Be smart. Get this fixed fast.

Learn your lesson and resolve the problem that caused the litigation. Then tighten up your processes to avoid these problems and move on.

Chapter 18

Things Managers really shouldn't do.

Sometimes we see reports on the television where managers show how their PR intellect is close to zero. I cringe to see theses events and I wish they never happened. Nevertheless, these groups managed to have PR meltdowns.

I use these three examples to show the idiocy and enbarrasing behaviour in different scenarios. How the hell did these people ever manage a convenience store never mind some common sense to manage a multinational company? I'll never know.

These stories are not fairy tales nor urban legends, but the events that will stay with the perpetrators for the rest of their careers. Enjoy.

Auto-meltdown.

When Obama was elected POTUS, he inherited an economy that was on meltdown. The US economy was diving like a Gold Medal Olympian, heading for the water.

Unfortunately the dive was going to the biggest belly flop in history.

Gas was at four dollars for the first time in history. A good result was not on the cards. The Auto industry was in particularly bad shape. The Big Three were almost on their funeral pyres. Their deadline for finding cash was days before they would have to go bust.
Millions of unemployed on the horizon.
Biggest industry in North America on the rocks.
Obama and his economic team offered to almost buy out the Auto Industry by obtaining shares of the companies then when things got better would sell back the share to the Automakers. The bosses of the big three Auto manufacturers were summoned to Washington to explain their situation and beg for the monies that they all needed. The ask was for 75 Billion dollars, bailed out by taxpayers. How did these

captains of the auto industry get from Detroit to Washington DC to ask for the bailout?

Private planes at 40 000$ a ride. Arriving with a tin cup to rattle in front of Congress, the industry really impressed the lawmakers. Three planes costing 120 000$ to take the CEO's on a round trip could have been bought for 1000$ round trip in Business Class. The PR was not kind, and the lawmakers were not happy with this effort to beg for taxpayer money while the Gulfstream 7000 was warming up its engines at Dulles. Be the manager that does not spend money unnecessarily. If I was a shareholder I'd be mad as hell. Remarkably the companies didn't change their procedures even after this PR disaster.

Another transport story.

This is a New York story involving Warren Buffett and Wall Street bankers. Not as expensive as the last monstrosity but maybe when translated into percentages it could be just as bad.
After a meeting held at an uptown hotel in Manhattan between Buffett and those big shot Wall Street lawyers and bankers, it was decided to travel down to Wall Street to finish the meeting and have a look around the facilities.
The lawyers and bankers called their limousines. They piled in and then the convoy left towards 5th avenue heading south for downtown Manhattan. On their arrival at the bank they noticed that Mr. Buffet was not with them. They assumed that he would be following them to the bank, so they all headed upstairs.

Opening the door, they found Mr. Buffett already installed in the Board Room, waiting for the group to arrive. Mr. Buffett had done what he always does in New York. He walked across the street to the Subway and paid a couple of dollars to go downtown. He arrived at Wall Street and walked over to the bank, then waited half an hour for the limousine caravan to arrive.

This is a real mans outlook on managing and respecting your owners and shareholders. Sure limousine companies need customers as every company does, but when the expense does not come close to being an intelligent alternative, let it go. Be smart.

Quebec Provincial Police.

In Quebec, Canada there are three police forces. They are divided between local, city police; Provincial Police; Royal Canadian Mounted Police. Each one has its own field of operations and responsibilities. One of the activities of the Provincial Police is to ensure the safety and smooth operations of the highway system in Quebec. The Province is responsible for the highways therefore their Police force takes care of any emergencies or crashes.

The Police Force has a very strong Union representing the member of the force. All employees of the Provincial Police are members of the Police Brotherhood, which negotiates the employment contracts of the Officers. Because of these negotiations they are well paid with double dipping allowed, they enjoy early retirement and handsome pensions. During one of its negotiating periods the Union demanded that the members could work at a second job while they were not on duty. The Government negotiator agreed this to. It turned out to be a bad idea.

On March 14, 2017 there was a snowfall warning for the Montreal area. There had been a forecast of 20 centimeters of snow starting mid-morning to late evening. The storm had different ideas. It decided that it would start mid-afternoon and go on to midnight and eventually dump over 30 centimeters on the Montreal Urban area. This kind of storm is an easy operation for the snow blowers, ploughs and staff at the ready. Everyone in Montreal was waiting for an early day of work. We all knew that the storm was going to show up, but with the mid-morning no show, people were naturally getting a little nervous. The roads were clear until around three pm. Weekday traffic in Montreal usually gets busy around 3pm. Then there is a bulge around 4pm and tend to die off between 5:30 and 6:30. So it takes around 3 hours for all the traffic to get home. At 3pm every business, office, school, and everyone else decided that to avoid the storm all the employees were sent home. So, the whole mass of traffic was hitting the road home at the same time. The roads went from clear to standstill gridlock on all the highways around Montreal.

Then the snow decided that this would be a great time to dump what it had. Disaster. Snowploughs can't get through. Roads almost blocked, but passable if you waited. I was on the road from downtown to 20 kilometers north west of the city. It took 4 hours. An average of 5 kms an hour.

Many highways were difficult to navigate and the storm tested the high end of the capacity of the operations to deal with all the problems presented. Unfortunately the drivers and passengers on Highway 13 were not in luck. The highway runs north south just east of the Montreal airport. The southbound lane has an upward gradient that can be slippy. There were three trucks in the three lanes heading south. They got stuck on the same part of the gradient. The road was blocked. The Provisional Police showed up to fix the problem. The truck drivers refused to be towed because there was a fee of 1000$ to move them off the highway. The truckers reported that they were not at fault so why should they pay a fee.

Stalemate.

This was around 7pm. There were 500 cars stuck behind the trucks. The cops called their boss, to find a solution, but he said that he was busy with other things. 14 hours later the Police and Firefighters were able to get the 500 cars and the three trucks were excavated from the highway. Government officials, the Mayor, the Police Chiefs were apologetic and couldn't understand what happened. The car occupants kept their cars running to stay warm, but soon ran out of gas. They were cold, hungry and afraid. By 8am the next morning they had extracted almost all the afflicted.

The Police Officer or manager, who was responsible for this situation was a no-show, and not reachable. He was moonlighting on his double dipping job, of being a Real Estate Agent and was busy at the closing of a property instead of looking after a possible disaster of a situation. The Brotherhood defends him and the public is astonished. This is a précis of the situation. But really? Would you as a senior manager like to see this happen to one of your subordinates. Opening double dipping to people with responsibilities is a dangerous game.
My advice is easy.

Don't let it happen.

You will get the blame if something goes wrong.

And it will.

The incompetence of these groups of people added to their so-called title of manager shows a complete disdain to all clients past, present and future.

The capacity to treat those they represent (their clients) as dirt is open for all to see and to make those clients decisions on the quality of these scoundrels is astounding. The so called masters of management in North America are generally not aware of a sound behaviour towards not only their shareholders, but of any potential customers they may wish to solicit.

Chapter 19

Building a team.

Any team required to build a department from the outset requires the same set-up. A good mix of experience, knowledge, vision, youth and a reasonable mandate.

Young companies, like todays disrupters, are infused with youth. Energy abounds. Traditional management where there is a healthy mix of young and old makes to ensure success of an organisation.

Youth is good. Motivation is plentiful. A 30 year old looking at a long-term post will be there for 30 years. Some new hires may see little chance to get to the top despite their experience and could be lost. Good employees may not want to hang around for a chance they are not certain to realise.

Mature, experienced staff is like a control rod in a nuclear reactor. They can cool things down. Balance the unit with young, old and in between. You may hear the experienced manager say, 'Great Idea on paper. We tried this at ABC Telecoms, and it was a total disaster because of X, Y and Z.' Mature employees can be mentors for the young people in the social graces of employment. They can offer context and show younger employees reality checks that they have experienced.

It's like the Mature Elephant problem in South Africa. Where there is a lack of maturity, then hanky-panky is the order of the day.
The elder of the tribe is still revered in society. Younger employees are gung ho and want to get to the prize very quickly. Their sense and perception of time is that speed and accuracy are important. It's OK to make mistakes, if we learn from them. Our seniors have experienced more mistakes. In your culture, generate a 'bounce your ideas off of an elder's thinking.' You may be surprised.

Tendencies seem to be evolving around youth. In Canada, Justin Trudeau is the Prime Minister. 42 years old. Valerie Plante, Mayoress of Montreal, 39 years old. Jacinda Ardern, PM of New Zealand, new mother and 37 years old. This is the time of youth.

Young managers and entrepreneurs will look for the smartest and savant people with the best tech knowledge available. This doesn't bide well with those over 40. Keeping aware of technical advances is a must. There is a space for older employees. They have the knowledge of people and experience. This demographic can occupy the space which communicates with people and not AI. They have experience, which young Turks have still to taste.

Hire a manager who comes from another industry. She will bring an optic, which the other managers will not have thought of. General Managers who have worked in several industries bring a wealth of experience. Their ideas are generally flexible and well proven. If you inherit one, and they pick up fast, guard them well and learn from them.

This practice is dangerous to a certain point. Often Political Parties when they create their administration or Cabinet politicians are placed in charge of departments. There is very little correlation between the capacities of these appointees and the department given. You may see a schoolteacher in charge of the Ministry of Defence. You may see an ex-service officer in charge of the Ministry of Education! Every Political Party will do the same thing. They say that the idea behind all this is to show that the Minister, having no experience in his domain will be 100% objective to the tasks at hand.

This is as far from the truth as possible, and it can be proved every year. After six months to one year into their administration the managers of the Party will have a cabinet shuffle. Herein the schoolteacher will be sent to Health and the ex Officer to Industry. What nonsense. Objectivity be damned. Put the best man available for the job in the job. All this shuffling around doesn't promote expertise. It hides inaptitude and disasters. The same goes for any company.

A team mix

Teams need cool heads and many skills. A mix of ages, experiences and personality makes the best. If you have problems with personality or the skill sets required for the team. We will have the following social stereotypes all in the same workplace.

- Baby Boomers
- Generation X
- Millennial
- Generation Z

As a generalisation the demographic nomenclatures are clearly defined except for the Generation Z. Their definition is still being explored. Old style management is still, even these days the most effective. Communication between interested parties works the best. Give service to each other. Use each level to their capacity for understanding and doing their work. Don't expect the Baby Boomer to understand 100% what the GenZ is talking about. What is important is the transition of information that is important.

- I need 50k$ to deliver the product tested and confirmed.
- Marketing has defaulted on the project time line.
- Core Electronics have gone bust.

Inputs from all demographic levels are valid. The steady hand of an experienced manager. The innovation of a GenZ. The middle groups of GenX and Millennial who can be experts in the gaps, who have experiences in development, long term. They know the software from its beginnings. This knowledge is precious.

Learn what you can. The young from the old. The old from the young.

I do believe qualified general managers can manage almost anything.

A Government needs specialists. Each job is very heavy and is under scrutiny every day for every decision. The only scrutiny in our jobs falls to our Boss. The Government has to keep the people happy. We have to keep the Boss happy.

The armed forces have a general admission program for officers coming in with a University Degree. The degree can be in any discipline. The candidates are well briefed during the hiring process that the Degree has no relationship to the mandate given to the candidate. A Chemistry major could find herself in charge of the payroll. A Doctorate in Organisational Behaviour could be mandated to foreign weapon sales.

Many governmental entities follow the same route where any graduate with any certification can find herself in any specific office. The idea is of course to ensure the sound, level management of what is generally, one of the major expense centers in the country.

Tell everyone who reports to you that your expectation is that they all use Strategic Management methodology.

Test the team. Check the previous experience of managers.
Check written work, talk to previous coworkers. Give them a chance to prove themselves. If the person does not delivery quality the first time out, take over. The faster you detect a dud the faster you can move them to the door.

Most jurisdictions have a probationary period after hiring where there is a prescribed period that you can open the door for a dud without any repercussions. Be fast and firm on this. Moving someone close to the door is difficult at the best of times. If you smell a dud, then act.

Chapter 20

Short and Sweet

Sales

The Sales Department.

CEO. 'Good Job Charlie. You had a good 4th quarter on sales for XYZ. What do you need for next years summer season?'

Charlie (VP Sales). ' Thanks Boss. I need a 25% add on to marketing budget for the XYZ. We expect an increase of 200% sales not including our California franchisees where we expect 300%.'

CEO. 'Done, expect the budget OK from finance before 4pm.'

Charlie. 'Thanks Boss.'

If you don't generate sales, the whole company is doomed.
No effort of any department in the organisation can live without the Sales Guys. The troops who will win the war and bring home the booty. Or will be ambushed and arrive home with their heads held low and no prizes to share with the rest.

If you have a sales department, which reaches the same level of sales every year, they are not doing their jobs. Sales must increase on a quarterly basis. Yearly increased are for losers. Yes. We have companies that have longer years, or cyclical demands but really, if you want to survive, constant improvement is a must.

If the Sales Manager misses his target the first year check his work. If he is on the wrong track tell him. If he misses the first quarter of his second year, move him to the door.

Time never stands still for the Sales Manager.
Of all the Managers, he is the one on the clock.

There are different Salesmen based on dollar value.
Who are the sales guys who are paid the most?

Wall St Bankers? Airplane Sales? Manhattan Real Estate?
Hedge Fund Managers? Leasing Oil Field land in Alberta?

Who knows? But I guess some of these are probably in there.
Who makes the deals?

Depending on the value of the deal, at the high end it will be first principals' head to head. One hundred Boeing 787's to Iran. This will be a deal between the Chairman and CEO of Boeing with the President or the Minister of Transport of Iran.

On the other end it will be the sales guy knocking on doors trying to get households to change their TV provider.
The commissions are different.
The higher you get up the ladder of sales the more influence and options are awarded to you to make the deal happen.

If I sold 100 Boeing 787's to Iran, and I had to tell the Boss that I discounted the sale at 5% to make the deal work, I'd still make the deal work. (This is an exaggeration. I would call the CEO first), still a huge number but for one hundred 787's I would still be one of the richest sales guy in the world.

If I was hitting a neighbourhood to sell TV subscriptions and I discounted the pricing by a penny I'd be out on the street.

Volume makes a great salesman. Good salesman can read the client. He knows which button to press to get the deal done.

Trump bullies people into deals.
Don't Bully.

I have experienced the hard sell many times in offices across the US. The product is shown to you. They surround you with a 2 to 1 ratio of salesmen and then the sales pressure is on. Awkward silences. Hard Stares. Sham hurt feelings to a refusal. Taking negative decisions as personal slights. All part of the game. Be honest but don't give them a PO unless you need it. Bullying the client for a purchase is common.

The pressure is on. Good Cop, Bad Cop. Snake Oil Salesman. You have sole access to this software. Our CEO wants to have Lunch with you. Tee time tomorrow? Tickets for the game this weekend?

This offer is only good for today-We have shown you all the advantages-What are you waiting for? Here is the contract-Sign here on the bottom line-this offer is only good for the next minute.

Respect works. Knowledge works. Know your product. Find the problem that your customer has and show him the product that will solve all his problems. Don't lie to your customer. He will find out. Then the company loses. If you are not sure, say so. Then find the answer and deliver it immediately. Second-guessing is dangerous. Get the good info. Be quick, but accurate.

If the sales department is on the ball then we all get the bonus. Don't get jealous when the Boss invites the sales department en mass to his golf course on a freebie. No deals, no meals.

As a salesman you may be working high or low volume.
Bridge engineering. Hospital construction, Aircraft Building could be involved in contract negotiations during years for one sale. Knowing the product by salespeople who are usually from those same industries. The future will be stable in the near future for big buys. Retail will lose many sales people.

Amazon and Wal-Mart will vie for the King of the World.

Who knows the portrait of 2030.

What will happen to the Sales Departments or will AI replace it all?

Contracts

Be careful with contracts. With everyone you contract with. Ambiguity is not a word you should wave around when you are negotiating a contract, whether it is a purchase, sale, employment, trade, or anything.

Protect yourself. Do not take chances.

If you use lawyers to write your contracts DO NOT let them draft a contract and then submit it to you for your perusal. They will squeeze the air and money out of you with rewrites, your approval, your disapproval, and their suggestions, late rewrites ..good grief.

In any contract make the following notes before you give the file to the lawyers or who ever drafts the contract. Even send your requirements to your supplier and have them draw up the contract. Then he gets to foot the bill with your wants.

- We have no liability on this contract
- Minimise late fees or penalties
- Balance of sale instalment paid on the 6th of the month or asset is returned
- A legal lien on the asset at the start
- There will be no change to delivery time unless there is a force major.

When you get the contract back read it carefully. Make your changes and send it back. One time. Depending on the severity of the contract, give it to the right person to supervise and follow up. Tell the manager only to call you if there is something not right. If he doesn't contact you, check up on her every two weeks. 'How is the McDonald file going?' Takes 2 seconds.

Skill requirements to be the Boss

There are skills that the Boss is required to have. Some bosses are blessed by having a natural affinity to have been armed with these assets. Others have to make the effort. The best way is to learn early to study and maintain those skill sets. All bosses have a good grip on the essential tools in their repetitoir. Many of you will have some or even all of them. If you are missing a few then learn how. There are professionals who will help you.

- Be capable of speaking in front of a crowd of 5 to 10000 people
- Show empathy
- Remember people's names
- Think before you speak
- Learn how to use a Memory Palace
- Get an internal and an external mentor
- Know how to identify and resolve cognitive biases
- Recognise a trend and catch the wave
- Recognise a bad trend and get off the wave
- Keep up with new technology to the point that you can understand what the IT guy is saying

Learning new Technology can be difficult for the older members of the payroll. Don't expect Charlie who at 60 years old will be able to perfect his capacity on the latest Salesforce or SAP platform. Technology has accelerated the evolution of the workplace. Once Quantum Computers become viable, then affordable, we may all get lost. Only the young ones understand and integrate the new without batting an eyelid. The young will overshadow the older members as innovation after innovation bulldozers over the last one. Keep up with the innovations in your sector. Read quality materials. The Economist. NYT. The Guardian. Bloomberg. Financial Times. Le Monde. China Daily. El Mundo and the précis of MSNBC and the WSJ.

Times are changing though and with the passage of baby boomers out of the workplace, illiteracy in technology will be redundant in ten years.

Never trust the Boss who calls you;

- My Friend
- Sir or Madam
- Buddy
- Any other seemingly friendly banter

The Boss that uses this way of addressing his subordinates either doesn't know she is degrading you or she does know. If she doesn't know then she is just ignorant. If she does know then watch out.

Step carefully when you go to her office. Make sure that you cross the t's and dot the i's when you submit your budget or that latest report. When she has to reprimand you for any reason, and you had believed her banter, it will come as a shock.

The Boss that uses friendly name-calling is unprofessional, ignorant and disrespectful. She thinks it brings the reporters closer and easier to manage. When a reprimand is needed the reporter will feel doubly bad. If there was a reasonable relationship with the Boss, it will surely be ruptured.

It is only a matter of time before it happens. Reprimanding someone for a half-baked report, then calling him or her Buddy does not work for anybody.

The more we pollute our subordinate relationships the more the hurt we cause and cement a bad relationship. If you ever experience this, look for a new Boss.

If your equals use the same language to address you, knock it on the head smartly. A simple 'I don't like that, please stop.' will work. My Friend is the worst. I have heard it said to employees and I have cringed at the spectacle.

Spot cognitive biases. This is not as difficult as it seems. There are some major biases that show up regularly and can be dealt with. Lesser known biases can sneak in and slow you up. Learn about them. There are many groups of biases which cloud together Get to know these groups.

Cognitive
Prejudices
Contextual
Media
Policing

Today's managers must have a basic knowledge of Biases. If not you will have difficulty in defending your positioning during negotiations whether sales, Unions, your own salary, anything at all in your daily business biases will show their shadow. We must be aware.

Chapter 21

Wanderings

In the past ten years there has been an explosion of start-ups and app ups. Blackberry has disappeared, then as if by magic, showed up again with a completely different business model. Amazon is swallowing anything that moves. Uber, AirBnB, Twitter, Facebook, you know them all. It used to be Bell, GM, GE, and Wells Fargo.

There has been a flow of young people into these sectors where huge campuses have appeared out of nowhere to occupy hip parts of cities. San Francisco, Chicago, Toronto, Austin, Seattle, Denver and Montreal are booming with the new economy. One-man operations to 5000 engineers. 100 000$ start ups to multi billion companies. How do you manage a department or the whole company in the new economy?

You manage like you would manage any other company or organisation. There are changings happening. With new opportunities and new thinking about our futures, Management is essentially the same. Communication. Sharing knowledge. Preparing the relief. Improving. Shaving costs. Increasing revenues.

Look at the companies that are booming. The ones who have changed industries. The disrupters. Look at the ones that have been around for a while. Microsoft, PayPal, Amazon, and Apple. Look inside these companies or their ilk and you will find similarities. The structures existing in ATT will be pretty darn close to a solid tech company today. Everything that I write about here can be applied there. My take on the disrupters is very clear. Management specialists didn't create these companies. Engineers, computer scientists, poets, artists and dreamers created them. Once their disruptive selves realised what they had in their hands and they reached out for help, it was the managers who answered the call.

Google to Eric Schmidt. Apple to Tim Cook. Good old management works.

The economy of disruption is shaking up industries everywhere. The industries, which are disrupted generally, have the same features. Uber and AirBnB have shown the weakness of the industries that they have overtaken.

- No inexpensive alternative
- Fragmented players
- No single protectionist authority in market
- Generally disagreeable experience

The strength in their business models is obvious and easy to understand;

- Less expensive
- App which is easy to understand
- Immediate payment to employees. (I call them this as they can be disciplined)
- No Cash needed.
- No jurisdiction is aware of problems in others
- Winning solutions rolled out to problematic markets

How do you think Uber is going to become profitable?

There will not be any change in management towards their final goals. Uber will be around for a very long time. They will settle into their existing markets and make peace with the local authorities. They have managers working across the world working to initiate and maintain policies to ensure the eventual goal of the business model.

Don't take this as gospel. I am not on the board of Uber. But I bet that I'm not far.

- Period of calm in the markets served
- Increase the number of drivers to saturate the area
- Increase fares slowly
- Reduce the drivers share
- Continue their relationship with Carnegie Mellon University
- Test and Perfect the auto drive car
- Produce the optimum number of auto drive cars
- Launch the auto drive cars in test markets
- Release the liability of having human drivers
- Clean up and maybe turn a profit
- Find similar apps and snap up market clones

Drivers are the largest liability in the organisation. 75 to 80 percent of revenues go to the driver. Is it any wonder that the auto drive car is a priority? I am certain that all forward-looking efforts are focused on this occurring in the near future. I'll bet my wife and kids that this is the end game for Uber.

During the Moving conventions in Montreal, I had the opportunity to speak to a Minister of Transport of a European Country. The séance was similar to a TED talk presentation with many contributors. He impressed me the most so I tracked him down and he candidly explained what would happen.

France has already announced that by 2040 no automobile will be sold in France unless the automobile is 100% electric or Hybrid. By 2050, all automobiles will be 100% electric.

By 2060, all automobiles will be auto drive cars. Humans will be disallowed to drive cars. There will be huge change in the cause and effect of automobile accidents and the science will prevail.

The only bump in the road would be the USA. Elsewhere every other country will accept this. The reasoning is simple. All auto drive cars will be regulated to behave exactly the same way. The only outlaw driver will be the human element. Once Governments realises that 99% of road deaths will be stopped immediately, including all drunk driving incidents, there is really no choice. Incidents of drivers in their own cars would be looked upon as cigarette smokers are today.

The USA would have the same difficulty as they do with guns. Even if the US authorities wanted this to happen, minorities would influence politics and donors related to an organisation that unfortunately seems to have more influence than their weight should. Bikers and RV drivers will be surely disappointed. Elsewhere in the world after 2060, if you wish to drive a car, it will be in a closed track for enthusiasts.

Don't make the mistake that management working in the disrupters are any different than any traditional companies. Their mandate is to maximise profits by increasing revenues and decreasing costs.

By the turn of 2050 we will see;

- No one will own a car. Any car on the road will be on subscription service.
- All Cars will be electric, not gas.
- All Cars will be driverless.
- All Cars will be managed by the same platform. The reason is easy. When all cars on the roads have the same software then the only problem would be human drivers who could not control with the same software.
- 34 000 souls will be saved every year without car accidents.
- Drunk driving disappears.
- Or Climate Change will change our environment to accelerate the atmosphere to the point of no-return and poison the world.

Chapter 22

Culture

Do you know the culture in your organization? Where does it come from? Is it healthy? How do you change it, if it needs change?

The culture of any organization is the atmosphere at work. It is an invisible cloud, which cloaks every element of human resource. It surrounds every aspect of the workplace. What would you like to have in your company culture? Wealth. Respect. Honesty. Responsible. Happiness. Productive. Precise. Generous. These are some elements a mature organization should consistently strive for.

What do we not want in a culture? Laziness. Tardiness. Make do. Disrespect. Cheating. Passing the blame. Cooking the books. Theft. Lying. Favoritism.

If your organization has any of these elements then you possibly need a new culture. If you operate with any of these negative culture elements then stop kidding yourself. Everyone will know and will copy your lead on maintaining that culture. The unofficial structures within the organization will be aware of the negative culture.

STOP.

If you can't stop because of your position within the hierarchy and are missing the necessary weight to start that change there are certain strategies available to you to kick-start change.

The competition will, if not suspicious of, be well aware of the culture in your daily. The correct culture will win in the long run only if there is a buy-in to the culture. Bad culture will be damaging to the bottom line.

Ne'er do wells will be attracted and bad practices will be looked over. The spiral down tends to be kick-started by this. It must be turned around at all costs or else the spiral will accelerate and the organization will be more and more damaged goods.

It is not the only reason that companies fail. Sleeping at the switch brings you down, whether you are a captain of industry, or a mom and pop operation.

Identification of the culture problem is easy to find. Having the capacity to change needs a hard hand and a plan of action. Once started you will need the buy-in of everyone to change from CEO to mail room.

Change is needed.

It could probably be the toughest project undertaken. You will need to make it happen or there could be an existential problem.

Our favorite pals Laziness and Procrastination cause bad culture. There is a difference between the two. To me, procrastinators really want to do the job. They don't have the tools or are afraid to ask. They need encouragement and close supervision until the penny drops. They can be changed. Laziness is just not good.

You get willful procrastination and they don't care. They have to be moved to the door.
You can be cursed upon by both beasts. The procrastinators will be the lazy ones who will try to poison the new hires. The only work the lazy seem to enjoy is trying to make everyone work like them.
The lazy ones will not care.

All the moves in the book to make things bad are used liberally by the lazy. Work not done. Reports not completed. But the greatest wrong is the entrenchment of bad work habits tolerated by management.

The use of cognitive biases from Naive Bias to Declinism. Managers who are not on the ball and allow these behaviors to exist have to face the reality of the culture and a cleaning is required.

You may have been unlucky enough to be involved or witness the culling during a culture change. It is not a pretty sight. The bad culture, which requires a quick turn around, will be done as an exercise under duress. There is nothing difficult about it. There is a blueprint. The hardest part is swallowing the pill.

Culture Change Play List

1) Realize that you have this problem and bring all management on board.

2) Examine what needs thrown out, kept, and redone. All the nastiness must be removed. Illicit processes, mollycoddling, favoritism, lack of accountability eradicated by the will of the organization.

3) Tell the Union, if there is one, what's coming.

4) New operations manuals for everyone, every process rewritten.

5) Rewrite all HR manuals. Incorporate your values, Have everyone in the organization sign off on the new and the out of the old.

6) Start the new culture with the new hires. Values of respect, knowledge, productivity, and honesty installed at hiring. They are the vanguard of the new structure.

7) Identify and remove the sources of the old culture. Give the guardians of the old culture the opportunity to leave or to stay. The lazy will leave of their own accord once the process starts.

8) Cull the managers who do not support 100% the change.

9) Communicate every day to staff the ongoing changes to the organization once supporters of the previous culture have been culled. The replacements will be on board with the new culture with the changes in place.

10) Be truthful to yourself. Are you doing all you can? Are there shaky moments? Do you need outside help? If so, get an expert in. On occasion, we need outside expertise. Don't be shy to ask for help.

11) Never stop communicating the wins of the organization. Send emails every week to all the employees that our values are and our insistence on the respect of those values.

12) Create PR wins within the industry. Show your competition the changes made when recruiting. Find good people.

13) Monitor the culture. Be on guard. Protect it. Use surgery to remove any return to the old ways.

14) Hit hard the culprits who don't buy into the new culture.

Companies today are reeling over incidents within their culture, which were accepted and tolerated. These behaviors existed incognito for many years, embedded in the culture, but probably not spoken about, ignored and accepted.

Sexual Harassment has blown open the cultures of many household names and organizations and even in whole industries. Hollywood, TV, Ford factories and Sports to start with. We will be exposed to more and more as time goes on in all communities as Hospitals, Universities, and Armed Forces.

Another despicable culture trait is Racism. Even with professional HR embedded in an organization, Racist so-called jokes are accepted. Ignorance is no excuse. Call out the racist. Call out the sexist. If you don't then you own the open problems.

The culture must support all those affected. Zero tolerance of harassment or another offence should not be the rigid policy. It implies that you have one chance. Commit the offence and you are finished. My experiences in managing have shown me that zero tolerance policies will always end with a cry of unfairness.

There has to be a process and a chance for all to reach a level of sensitivity that pulls in the wrongdoer and makes the victims whole again. There will be different levels of guilt or innocence and the culture must support itself with these characteristics;

Every member of the organization must also be a member of the culture police when #me-too incidents are exposed.

Initially small incidents should be policed by co-workers, who rectify the immediate offence. A Racial joke or comment should be called out with. 'Stop! I will call HR.'

If you let it go, and allow it proceed past the first few words you are as guilty as the perpetrator.

The initial incident should go to your immediate supervisor, not HR. Based on the facts he will make the report with HR, possibly with you.

- Use 'STOP, I WILL CALL HR ' in any cases of verbal, non-solicited comments including;
- Racism
- Weight
- Sexual Harassment
- Job Performance
- Dress
- Bullying
- Intelligence

This could be used in the unofficial communications of the organization to help keep enforce the official.

Written, verbal, or physical harassment MUST go to HR.

Each incident will have its own parameters and facts.

Witch-hunts, burning people at the stake or trumped up courts cannot be used. A sensible, fair procedure managed by HR to ensure that the final decision is fair, firm, fast and de rigeur.

Micro Management.

Please, I beg you. Do Not Micro Manage ANYONE.

I understand that you want to know what's going on. You want to check if Charlie has finished deliverable VyWtX/avr/10-12 and if the costing is correct. Charlie will think that you are busting his nuts. Charlie is right.

You gave the job to Charlie. You told him the deadline. You gave him the parameters of the costing. You told him to call you if there was anything out of the ordinary.

He hasn't called you. Don't bust his nuts. If there is a problem he will call you.

Your behaviour as a manager has to be consistent. You do not yell. You do not disparage. You do not complain. You do not micro manage them.

If need be you will go and see Charlie to look at the problem if he needs help. You should know how to remedy the problem or least know who can. Then help Charlie fix the problem.

If Charlie had called and exposed a problem and got grief from you, how do you think Charlie would feel about calling you if he has a subsequent problem?

Charlie would be calling others to try and fix something that you are not aware. This line of communication must stay in place where your reply of 'Thanks for letting me know' for all cases shows an openness and an even demur, open to communication.

All calls to subordinates and the high ups should end like this.

We gave him the job. Let him do the job. After all he wouldn't be there unless we had faith in his capacity to finish what was asked of him.

Never interfere with subordinate work, or think your doing a favour for them by showing how smart you are for mundane work methods.

If the employee reports directly to you then at your next scrum expose the method as slow and expensive then change the method. If the employee reports to a manager that reports to you, then call the manager quickly, but tell him not to micro manage, but change the methodology rather than embarrassing the employee.

The End of the End.

What I've always found curious is that in most developed countries there is always a leftover of almost defunct industries with few members that have a larger than their numbers influence on Government policies. Farming for example has a strong influence even though a very small part of the population still farms. Grants, protected pricing, guaranteed subsidies are prominent in every market. Their influence is huge compared to their numbers. Tariffs are looked favourable for farmers while other industries are not.

The trade unions have been decimated over the recent years yet still hold sway over Governments. Smaller though their numbers are now they have maintained strength far exceeding their numbers. With the ever-accelerating modern economies based on technology and service industries shifting what will the next industry to be decimated?

The transport business with the introduction of driverless vehicles will see another industry, like farming, lose the employees and leave a select few in control of the industry.

There is a legacy of these industries that were once important and powerful. Farming has been automated with small populations in farming areas being capable to farm huge tracts of land. They are subsidised by governments to ensure that even during droughts or missed quotas there are dollars dropped to the sector.

Even though through innovation in the agriculture industries which allowed huge scales of economy and left hundreds of thousands, if not millions of farm hands out of the industry, the few still there have harvested huge benefits, and still command a strong presence in government affairs.

The steel business, shipbuilding, coal mining and other industrial industries which peaked in the early to mid 20th century, declined in many cities that were the engines of every Country. With the passing of these industries to service ones, the Unions left behind have still maintained a strong relationship towards political parties to help maintain policies.

I visited the Guinness brewery in Dublin, Ireland. Guinness is one of those worldwide beers that have become over the centuries omnipresent. I have never been unable to buy a pint of Guinness anywhere that I have travelled. It is only brewed at this one brewery in Dublin. During a tour of the brewery it was explained by the escort that the brewery used to employ 10 000 workers. I cheekily asked how many worked there now, and the reply was five in white lab coats who press buttons.

All industrial processes are heading that way.

In the very near future our lives are changing. The wave is already moving and its crest is getting larger and larger.
AL will make decisions for us in all our activities. Everytime you look for anything online. Everything you purchase. Every feature you request on your car. Every trip you make on every airline you use. Everything you eat and drink. Every movie and TV shows that you watch. Everything you read. Every comment you make.

Algorithms will decide what content you see. Decide what Your choices are for food, vacations, porn channels, books, toothpaste, beer, cars, clothes, schools for your kids, universities, make-up, Where to live. Your politics. This is the tip of the iceberg.

Be aware of the Algorithms. They will control all your choices, by showing what it thinks you need and nothing else. Targeting content to your history makes for an easier sale point.

As technology becomes more AI friendly more algorithms will become more exact and omnipresent.

The waves of technology can be overwhelming but you don't have to be an expert on every new development. Be at the least knowledgeable about new technologies, and especially if they affect directly your industry. Know enough to have reasonable conversation about new innovations.

Block chain is a good example. You don't have to know the internal workings of the technology needed, but knowledge of how it can reshape the industry you work in is needed. Don't be shy to call in consultants and have them keep your people up to scratch.

Innovations tend to be difficult enough when introduced. After a few months everyone should be fluent on the new technology, but not necessarily on the nuts and bolts. The result is what is important. You are a manager and it's the results by which you are measured.

Block chain is a distributed ledger recording a history of transactions across a network of computers. What makes block chain so special is that records can be distributed to participants securely and can't be manipulated. No one entity controls the network and transactions can be executed with less reliance on a central party.

As I said if you work in programming, or if you're looking at how your company could use it, then absolutely get to know the mechanics of block chain.
If you aren't – don't lose any sleep.
Everyone thinks that it's really important to understand the actual technology.
Nothing is further from the truth.

We can work with a mobile phone with hundreds of applications that are used for business. We don't need the knowledge of the inner workings. Just the result.
Block chain will change the commercial transaction market forever. There will be a few start-ups that will undoubtedly be consolidated in short thrift, to one or two huge corporations.

Do your job.

Let your Boss in what is going on.

Optimize your time.

If you need help, ask.

Always be learning.

Don't listen to Backstabbers or Big Gobs.

Be Firm, Fair and Fast.

Watch for ballooning Operational Budgets.

Do not tolerate Intelligent, but Lazy employees.

Stop any non-productive or negative cash flow procedures.

Hire the Best People.

Smile.

Know your employees, their names, and their functions.

Do not have more than five employees whom report directly to you.

If you are sitting at your desk and have no immediate task to do, you are wrong. Do it. Now.

Do not shoot the bearer of bad news. It takes strength to tell the Boss the truth.

Know the marginal value of what you contribute to the business.

www.ingramcontent.com/pod-product-compliance
Lightning Source LLC
Chambersburg PA
CBHW051321220526
45468CB00004B/1446